Breakfast with Salamanders

SEASONS ON THE APPALACHIAN TRAIL

ALAN RICHARDSON

DAIYUPEAK
PRESS

Copyright © 2021 Alan Richardson
All rights reserved
Daiyu Peak Press | Waltham MA

This publication may not be reproduced, sorted in a retrieval system, or transmitted in whole or in part, in any form or by any means, electronic, mechanical, photocopying, recording, or otherwise without the permission of the author.

THE APPALACHIAN TRAIL

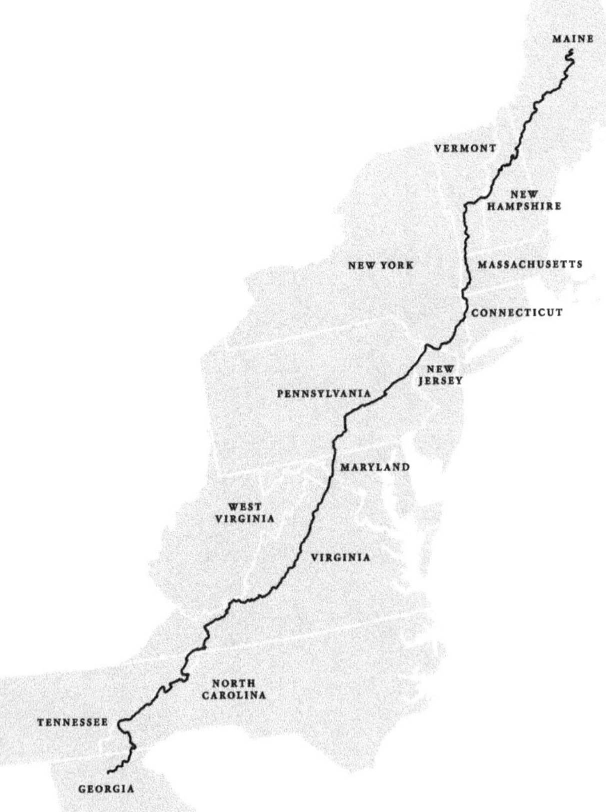

IN MEMORY OF

DAVID W. RICHARDSON

APRIL 20, 1924 - APRIL 23, 2011

CONTENTS

PREFACE

Achieving artistic excellence, each holds one attribute in common:
each remains attuned to nature throughout the four seasons.
Whatever is seen by such a heart and mind is a flower,
whatever is dreamed is a moon.

Matsuo Bashō, *The Knapsack Notebook*

On a bright morning in the middle of August I found myself on top of Katahdin, the highest peak in Maine and the traditional end point—and toughest climb—of the Appalachian Trail. While a handful of fellow hikers posed and cavorted on the iconic sign marking the summit, I walked some yards off to another marker, equally iconic but for some reason attracting no attention apart from my own. Tall, imposing, a little precarious looking, the cairn stood out against the high clouds floating in from the north, rich granite shades of green, grey, and red set off against the ash grey backdrop. As I drew near to the rough pyramid of stones, mostly local, a few carried here from distant places, I fought down rising tears. There was an offering to make.

This account of hiking the Appalachian Trail differs from others you may have encountered. Apart from the 100 Mile Wilderness and Katahdin, which I saved for last, I backpacked the entire AT out of order. Starting in the White Mountains of New Hampshire, which have practically become my back yard, I hop-scotched my way both north and south, not even glimpsing Springer Mountain, the traditional starting point in Georgia some 2,185 miles south of Katahdin, till I had already covered well over a thousand miles of white-blazed trail. As a result, this book does not follow a predictable line, as do almost all other AT books, whether from south to north or north to south, whether accompanied or solitary, whether tragically interrupted and then heroically resumed or doggedly, blessedly unbroken from start to finish. Split up into forty-seven different trips, ranging from overnights in New England to a long trek in Virginia that filled most of one October, my hike proceeded haphazardly, guided by convenience and sheer whim, moving in fits and starts. Instead of resolutely marching in one direction or another, I jumped and danced around.

My hike was not an epic but a miscellany, a crazy quilt, a collage.

Looking back, I would not have had it any other way. Hiking the AT in sections, rather than "thruhiking" it from end to end, allowed me to experience the trail in every season and in all weathers, from a parched 150 mile slog through New Jersey and New York during a freakishly hot week of May, to snowshoeing up the north face of Mt. Moosilauke through three feet of powder one frigid Christmas Day. Hiking in all seasons meant seeing an unusual variety of mosses and wildflowers, birds and mammals (including a few memorable fellow hikers), and nearly every atmospheric condition you might imagine. Sometimes I had to ford waist high streams during rains that refused to let up, sometimes I enjoyed a week or more of cool, sunny weather; I hiked in temperatures from single digits to the high nineties, and twice I narrowly dodged being struck by lightning. Each day brought a different kind of challenge and a different kind of beauty. I aimed to savor it all.

In the eleven years I spent section-hiking, I saw the Trail change. It grew more popular and more crowded and sadly, much more subject to abuse. Solitude, easy to come by during the early years, became an occasional luxury by the end. Naturally, I also saw myself change. I went through a divorce, watched my kids grow up, lived through my father's decline and death, and had to come to terms with my own aging process, hard to ignore when you're regularly testing your strength and stamina. I also returned to the formal practice of Zen Buddhism, which I had left behind three decades before, and inevitably my Zen practice and my hiking practice flowed together. This book is not, however, "Zen and the Art of Hiking the Appalachian Trail": my focus throughout remains on nature, on what the ancient Chinese called "mountains and rivers." Poets in the Zen tradition from Han Shan in eighth-century China to Bashō in seventeenth-century Japan to Gary Snyder today do not, of course, separate the intimate experience of nature from what today we might call the "spiritual," any more than did, in our own great American vein of nature writing, Thoreau or Muir. (Or, among the British Romantic poets I teach and write about for a living, Wordsworth or Shelley.) Looking gratefully to all these traditions for inspiration, I have tried to give a sense of what mountains and rivers and the footpaths that wander through them can still mean to us at a time when the concept of nature is being challenged and the natural environment itself has come under unprecedented stress.

I have encountered much disagreement over the years about what exactly counts as hiking the entire Trail, so I should make my own approach, or if you prefer, ethic, clear. For me, it was important to pass every white blaze, that is, the ones that were there to be passed as I hiked a given section. (The Trail changes every year through long term relocations and sometimes every few weeks through short term work arounds; in the eleven years I hiked it, the overall length itself changed from 2,173.9 when I started in 2004 to 2,189 miles when I finished in 2015, and my personal mileage total ended up at 2,178.7, though I would not swear to the accuracy of that figure.) I also wanted to spend as many nights in the woods as I could fit in, and so I did every mile wearing a full backpack. Others have found it more practical or more enjoyable to day hike parts of the Trail, to occasionally "slack pack" (walking with a light daypack while one's backpack is hauled up the trail by car), to "blue blaze" (making use of alternative trails or parallel roads on occasion), even to "yellow blaze" (jump ahead to a Trail town or road crossing by hitchhiking or taking a shuttle). Trail runners, looking to set unofficial (and meaningless) speed records, go so far as to rely on mobile support teams. None of these methods interested me.

Which is not to say I didn't receive a great deal of support. I remain especially grateful to those who took me to and from trailheads—Ash and Kim Nichols, Brian Richardson, Joel Dando, the late Jim McGavran, Dawn Rockwell, Leon and Jessica Hayward, and Joni Syrotick. Thanks as well to those who read and commented on this book in progress, especially Ash, Brian, Pierce Butler, and Suzanne Matson. And of course, deep bows to the great web of Trail and shelter maintainers, inn and hostel keepers, shuttle drivers, "Trail angels," and others whose selfless, unglamorous, devoted labors make it possible for us all to keep hiking.

FALL

In mountain groves, grasslands, and woods the truth has always been exhibited.

Hongzhi Zhengjue, "Self and Other the Same"

September 2004. Not five minutes from my car I'm stopped short. After two days of rain (the skirts of Hurricane Ivan), the Oliverian Brook is running high—the step stones across it gleam greenly under six inches of rushing water. And the heavily eroded bank angles down so steeply that there's nowhere to sit and take off my boots. So I scramble back up, digging my toes into the steep, wet earth until I hit flat ground just feet from the highway, startling a great blue heron that, oddly enough, has chosen to cross the road on foot. Now that I'm here I return to my car in the parking area where I can sit while I change boots for hiking sandals. I push my socks deeply into my boots, tie the boots to my backpack, cross the asphalt and work my way back down the bank, this time digging my heels in. And, about to cross, I stop myself again—the water is moving fast and I'm going to need a stick.

All the loose wood on the bank has long since rolled into the brook, so it's back up to the highway, ignoring the sign directing me to the high water bypass detour—if the Trail goes across the brook, I go across the brook—and into the woods behind my car. Right away I find the perfect hardwood branch, reasonably straight, solid (I test it by banging it hard against a hunk of granite pushing out of the ground), over four feet long. With the stick I find it easier to negotiate the steep bank, and now at last I ease my legs into the stream. The morning has started out cool and rainy and the chill in the brook water runs from my feet right up to my brain like a jolt of adrenalin. Just as well because even with the stick the crossing demands all my awareness, the force of the water changing every few instants, the submerged stepping stones mossy and treacherous. Half way across, the big rocks underfoot give out and I'm suddenly in up to my thighs. I wrestle one leg against the current into the deepest, fastest part of the brook and as I raise the other foot I nearly go over, the oak branch and two quick hops saving me from an ignominious dunking. A few colored leaves ride the current behind me and circle for a bit in the eddy that nearly took my legs from me as I step-stumble the last few feet to the north bank. The rain lightens as I dry my feet with the tops of my socks and get my boots back on for the long climb, about 3750 feet of elevation gain, to the summit of Mount Moosilauke.

It hardly sounds like a promising start to my first Appalachian Trail section hike, yet as the first hour passes and the rain lets up altogether, this begins to feel downright auspicious. I've set out despite the rain, seen an improbable heron (a refugee from the storm?), forded my first tricky stream, and now reap my reward of clearing skies and glistening woods. The eight miles leading from NH 25 over Moosilauke to Beaver Brook shelter give me a taste of much that I'll encounter on many section hikes to come in New England. Dense, largely deciduous woods to start with, oaks, maples, and beeches, rain still dripping off the changing leaves and earthy scents rising from the damp ground. Then a little road walking before crossing a much smaller stream into fallow fields where the path skirts along the edges of untended cropland, long grasses wetting my calves as I hike along the beaten down path. Then, at last, the fields give way to a steep jumble of rocks and roots as the real climbing starts, not to let up till the summit.

According to the almanac, it's a few days shy of autumn, but here in New Hampshire the season is already in full swing. This feels appropriate, since for me the season of new beginnings has always been fall rather than spring. Maybe because, first as a student and then a teacher, I have long lived by the academic calendar, or maybe because leaf change and the coming of cooler weather has always felt refreshing, vibrant, a time of renewal. I hike best, especially if I'm climbing, in a temperate zone of 30°-60° F, so I'm grateful for the cool, overcast day as the path grows steeper. As anyone knows who has staked out a tent here, there's not much soil over the rock in northern New England, and between water erosion (the trails tend to turn into streams in heavy rain) and the wear of innumerable boots, you soon find yourself climbing up rocks as you gain much elevation. The hike up Moosilauke is no exception. The rock here, dark-colored grainy schist with glints of mica and occasional pale gleams of quartz, gives good purchase, despite the lingering wetness from the morning rains. I move quickly, passing up a young dayhiker couple, perhaps Dartmouth students climbing a mountain that their College owns, odd as it seems that anyone but the gods could lay claim to such a place as this.

The southernmost of the White Mountains, Moosilauke features a progression of forest types characteristic of many ascents to come. First the hardwoods make room for more and more evergreen trees, with prickly black spruce and sweet-scented balsam fir gradually coming to dominate, eventually leaving room only for the occasional paper birch, its white bark peeling in places and revealing the pinkish brown skin beneath. Then, still higher up, the spruce and fir trees grow shorter until finally, near the rock scramble to the summit, they absolutely dwarf, in places even growing horizontally, carpeting the rocks. Krumholz—German for "bent" or "crooked" wood—represents the evergreens' last best hope to survive the fierce winds and operatic temperature changes that mark the high places in the White Mountains. Thanks to the unusual confluence of three weather systems, from the west, from the South Atlantic, and from the cold Canadian north, the mountains here boast some of the most dramatic weather in the world, and I have to be ready today for anything from Indian summer to early snowfall. Blasted by the boreal winds the trees peter out altogether at only 4500 feet, half a mile short of the summit, while in Washington State I remember reaching timberline at a more reasonable 6000 feet of elevation.

And so at last, pulling myself up a succession of steep rock slabs, I leave even the krumholz behind and find myself in an austere alpine meadow, one of the lowest elevation alpine zones on the globe. The harsh weather does not allow for dramatic floral displays like the bright gold glacier lilies and lurid pink monkey-flowers of the North Cascades. Instead, you find delicate, miniscule flowers embedded in low growing, tiny-leaved plants, with names like Alpine Azalea, Mountain Cranberry, and Alpine Goldenrod. Today, though, only a scatter of miniature white flowers can be found in bloom, the unglamorous and tenacious Mountain Sandwort. I stick rigorously to the narrow, sandy summit trail, careful not to stomp on any of these hardy yet fragile plants, which can take over a decade to recover from a single careless bootstep.

On the very top, at 4830 feet, I stop to rest on one of the large, eroded, squared off granite chunks that make a kind of fallen Stonehenge around the summit sign. These once formed the base of an inn, the Prospect House, that burned down in the 1940s, never to be rebuilt. Moosilauke makes for a heartening story to all who love wildness: the west slopes, once clearcut, now densely reforested, the tourist hotel gone, the summit area once more a home for alpine shrubs and snowshoe hares, lichens and white-throated sparrows.

Now the old foundation stones blend in with the surroundings, and the broad carriage road has long ago dwindled to a rocky footpath. May the top of Mt. Washington one day look the same!

On a cloudless day, Moosilauke offers stunning views on all sides and one can see hundreds of neighboring peaks, including many on the Appalachian Trail: the four Franconia Ridge mountains to the northeast and, behind them, the Northern Presidentials—Washington, Adams, and Jefferson; due east, the Bonds, Carter Dome, and the Wildcats; Smarts Mountain and Mount Cube to the south; looking west, Killington and Breadloaf in the Green Mountains of Vermont; and Mount Wolf and the twin peaks of the Kinsman Ridge close ahead to the north. But today rainclouds hem in the summit, so I make only a quick stop, continuing north and down the far side of the mountain a couple of miles to Beaver Brook shelter. The lean-to has been taken over by a passel of kids who wait impatiently for their dads, a quartet of jovial, beer-bellied firemen, to make their way up the shorter but steeper trail from the north.

I set up my tent on a narrow site cut into the mountain side overlooking the shelter, wishfully eyeing a more removed site just above it that's already been staked out with a tent still smaller than my own. The tent's owner, Hippie Long Stockings, a strong, pretty young woman sporting signature dirty blond braids, turns out to be an inveterate distance hiker. She's already done the AT at least once and seems to be spending much of the current year hiking it in both directions from various jumping off points. Over the next few years I'll read her entries in a number of shelter registers spread widely over the Trail, immediately identifiable from the colored pens and stickers she uses, and several times I'll find myself within a few days of her, though I'm fated never to see her again. However, something Hippie says changes all my AT hikes to come. Preparing to break out my elaborate, weighty ceramic filter, I ask her if she treated her water—she says that, between the high altitude we're at and the way the stream is flowing, she saw no reason to bother. I remember all the water I drank straight from streams and springs in the Cascades and decide to leave the filter in my backpack: it's the last time I carry it. The water from Beaver Brook is cold and delicious and does me no more harm than will countless high altitude springs and streams to come.

At night the boys in the shelter settle down gratefully early and I have a chance to sleep in peace, rain pattering gently on my tentfly, the brook running musically within hearing. I'm still not used to sleeping alone in the woods, though, and I'm visited by nightmare, dreaming that some varmint with teeth like broken glass, a weasel or even a wolverine, has clamped its spring-loaded jaws onto my right hand. I wake up to find that same hand constricted and half numb, so I turn over and listen to stream and forest sounds for the next hour or so. From childhood till my early twenties, I must have slept in the woods at least a couple hundred times, but I had never slept alone—without a buddy, a father, or a brother either sharing the same tent or in another within arm's reach—before a month earlier, on a "practice" overnight. That night some gigantic beast ran circles around my tent for over an hour after midnight, crashing through bushes, snapping off branches, and plunging into a nearby pond with a monstrous splash: the next morning I found moose tracks encircling my makeshift tentsite. Tonight's nightmare at least comes honestly.

The rain has tailed off by morning and I'm the first out of the shelter area, climbing back up to the summit as I return on the same stretch of the AT I've come by. But today it's a whole different trail. Just a few hundred yards above Beaver Brook I find myself inside the clouds that have entirely blanketed the mountaintop. Nearing the summit area, hiking along rocky ledges where the fir and spruce trees begin shrinking again, the dwarf trees sparkle in the soft light with thousands of ice crystals. Still higher up, I grow almost breathless, not from the climb but from the way the ice has built feathery outworks projecting from every available vertical surface—krumholz, rocks, even the summit sign. The entire summit has been transformed into a world of glistening, fantastically delicate frost sculptures pointing into the wind. Rime ice: millions of tiny, supercooled water droplets captured from the streaming clouds by any cold form projecting above the ground. Including my own form: I look down to see frost outworks clinging to my backpack, my parka, even my pants legs.

Swollen, streaming clouds
rush the chill summit. Rime ice
grows on rocks, trees, me.

The winds begin to gust so powerfully that one sharp blast rips the nylon cover off my backpack—I just manage to snatch it from the air before it sails away toward the Presidentials. I notice my hands growing numb inside my light hiking gloves and I start jogging toward the tree cover on Moosilauke's southwestern flank.

October 2005. Fall hikes nearly always had to be tucked into a weekend, three or four days at most, and shorter days at that. From my home base near Boston, however, trailheads in New Hampshire, Vermont, northern Connecticut, and even the Mahoosucs in Maine waited within three and a half hours by car. In the beginning I concentrated on Massachusetts, my adopted home state, where driving due west could get me to an AT parking area in as little as two hours.

Once Columbus Day had passed fellow hikers grew few and far between. Compared to New Hampshire, with its hundreds of peaks, or Vermont, with its local enthusiasts, Western Mass seems undervalued or at least underused. Also, with no elevation higher than Greylock (a modest 3490 feet), less risky, so I could more or less ignore the weather forecasts, which often proved wrong in any case. Thanks to the near miraculous new materials that had come into being since my youthful backpacking days, waterproof and breathable, light and warm, paper thin and durable, a brief downpour was nothing to fear and hiking in a light rain could be downright pleasant. Anyway, no one who grew up hiking in Washington State worries too much about rain.

Mostly I did out and backs from my car, having already learned from Moosilauke that you can never really hike the same trail twice. The return trip meant not just different weather and light conditions, but different vistas, different birds and animals, new things to notice—a rock shape from some other planet, a dead tree positively Gothic in its ominous decay—so striking that you could scarcely believe you'd missed them on the way out. But so it is: just turn around and a new world opens before your eyes.

I rarely shared a campsite or shelter on those fall hikes, excepting the occasional critter asserting its rightful claim to the forest. One cold midnight on Mount Wilcox in late October, sleeping with my rain jacket zipped over the foot of my sleeping bag, I woke up to find a deer mouse nosing its way under the parka in a desperate search for warmth. A hard rain beat on the shelter roof—perhaps the mouse's nest was flooding. I let it sleep next to me, making sure not to roll over, till some time later the little beastie started to bite its way through the sleeping bag, wanting to make a nest out of the warm down inside. One swift jerk of my right foot made for an instant eviction. I hiked out the next morning in a light snow that soon let up, a lovely rustic walk through marsh land and cow pastures, across the Tyringham valley, and past dreamlike Goose Pond, calmly reflecting the iron gray skies above. That day I saw not a single soul beside some chickadees, a downy woodpecker, and of course the cows, a slight shivering of their hides showing their disapproval as I made a path through the herd.

The year before, on a December hike north from Jug End to the Ice Gulch near Great Barrington, I find myself sharing an otherwise vacant shelter with a much more tenacious beast. Although I can hear the sounds of hunters, or rather their guns, crossing East Mountain, this turns out to be another day where I see no one at all on the trail, or rather, no other person. At one point a group of eight to ten deer glide across the trail ten yards ahead of me, moving out of range of the hunters. After them comes a group of late migrating birds, tiny ruby-crowned kinglets flitting south ahead of the first snow. What were they doing in New England so late in the year? Reaching my destination in good time, I climb down the trailless Ice Gulch, a jumble of titanic blocks of gneiss, projecting out of a deep cut in the hillside like an ancient, petrified wound and forming cave-like sunless hollows that harbor ice all summer long. Scrambling back up the slick boulders I can't help thinking of a poem I've taught to generations of college students—"A sunny pleasure dome with caves of ice!"—wondering if the avid walker Coleridge had ever bushwhacked his way to such a spot in the English Lake District, New England's geological twin. I've read that before the continents split apart, the two regions were in fact one: New England indeed.

I'd intended to sleep above the gulch, where a south-looking tent platform opens to a sweet view of the sunset, a skyfull of soft cold fire, but I find it hard to pass up the empty shelter, especially on such a short December day. So the platform serves for cooking and dining, a high bunk in the shelter for sleeping. A loud thump that seems to come from the shelter roof jars me awake at one in the morning. Shining my headlamp out the open side reveals nothing, though I hear some rustling in the leaves. Another hour and a half and I'm awake again, to the sounds of some forest creature scratching its way over the shelter edge and scrabbling around on the wooden floor. My headlamp now reveals a large porcupine skittering about on curved, bearlike claws. It shies a little at the light, but does not budge.

On short days I bring a small flashlight to back up the headlamp, and now I shine, jiggle, and flash both of them in the porkie's eyes to minimal effect. So I begin to scold it in a loud voice, even throwing in a few gratuitous insults. Nothing, and I have yet to learn that you should take a few plum sized stones to bed with you when you see the telltale signs of gnawing on the shelter frame. It stands to reason that porcupines would have little fear of other creatures—long needles guard it on all sides and give it a shaggy, disreputable air. Yet I like it—I feel almost honored by the unexpected late-night visit. More than that, I feel an uncanny sense of intimacy, sharing this small outpost in the dark, silent woods with such a wild and scraggy critter. It's come looking for salt and will happily chew on anything us unwashed hikers have left our briny touch on—luckily, I had known enough to take my boots up to the loft with me or he would have found their sweat-cured leather irresistible. Instead, he starts scrabbling at a support post, trying to get to my backpack, which I've hung high up to discourage rodents. Finally, needing to sleep again, I slide off the bunk to the floor and grab the shelter broom. Taking his time, the porcupine drops onto the ground and wanders back into his woods. I fall asleep listening to the dwindling scuttling sound as he moves through a wilderness of fallen leaves.

November 2004. The day starts out sunny and cool. The Trail keeps to the woods here, a nine-mile stretch between two picturesque New England towns (Monterey to the south, Tyringham to the north). I head toward Tyringham, through stretches of hardwoods and across a series of bogs, past Benedict Pond and then up a steep rocky scramble to the Ledges, where you can see as far as the Catskills. The path continues over Mount Wilcox, where the month before I let a mouse snuggle against me for warmth, and then zigzags through the Beartown Forest with its crumbling network of stone walls, the last remnants of a farming culture that died out more than a century ago. I wade through a caramel river of fallen leaves where the trail should be: wherever the white blazes fade out or dwindle, I stay on the path by imagining where I would go next if I were mapping it out for the first time.

The tentsite, at the end of a rocky, descending gulch, overlooks the bucolic Tyringham Valley. I worry that it's too close to the village, because of the noise (cows and pickup trucks) and because in the woods I feel safest when furthest away from road crossings—the harder it is to get to a campsite, the less likely that trouble will visit it. Yet the Shaker Campsite has a special draw, located among the foundation stones of a long abandoned Shaker settlement, dating from the heyday of that charismatic, childless sect. Perhaps some ecstatically dancing yet coldly celibate ghost will visit me tonight. I hang my food on a bear cable and introduce myself to the hiker who's taken the other tent platform, a quiet, bearded young man named Lightway. Half an hour later, as I gather armfuls of fallen sticks for a fire, Lightway wordlessly packs up and heads north into the valley. He'd mentioned doing most of his AT section hiking in November: I guess that he likes solitude at least as much as I do.

I came to backpacking alone by default, when I discovered that no one I knew wanted to come with me. Or with anyone else. As I talked with one friend after another who'd mentioned backpacking in the past, I let myself in for a litany of bad knees and back problems, heel spurs and torn ligaments. (I didn't even bother asking my wife, who liked to dayhike but refused to sleep on the ground; my kids expressed theoretical interest, but finding the time was another story.) I began to realize how lucky I was to have neared the age of fifty with a reasonably intact frame, perhaps because though I had always hiked, run, cycled, or swam, I had largely avoided athletic competition of any kind. Now a lifelong preference for endurance sports was paying off: my body itself had endured.

Almost immediately, during those early solo overnights in Western Mass, I didn't just get used to hiking alone—I began to crave it. I grew aware of what you might call a solitude deficit built over a decade and a half of marriage and child-rearing, keenly as I loved playing with my kids or just existing in the same house with them. And alone in the woods I saw more, heard more, savored more. Without companions, far from electronic distractions (my cell phone stayed scrupulously off), I had a chance to listen to the woods and to some of the long neglected voices in my head. They had, it turned out, a lot to say.

And yet sleeping alone in the woods still took some getting used to. Too many years, perhaps, of Boy Scout indoctrination in the "buddy system," a post World War II innovation in stark contrast to the great American tradition of going it alone: Boone, Thoreau, Muir, Abbey, and the early Scouts themselves, who often as not did their first twenty-miler solo. My aging Dad couldn't hide his concern every time I mentioned an overnight coming up: "You're not going alone, are you, Al?" Yet Dad, who'd grown up wandering and camping out in the Montana hills, more than anyone else had shown me how you could feel secure and at ease in the woods. Why, then, did the nightmares still come?

This night in the woods begins with eerie sounds that stir more than frighten me: the howling of a coyote pack from somewhere across the valley, a weird wild singing that bypasses my brain to resonate in my gut, which registers both wariness and a mysterious kinship. As the night wears on the coyotes wake me up repeatedly, sometimes from far away, sometimes nearby—I don't mind them. Unfortunately, the yard dogs down in the valley have their own opinion, kicking up a racket that, along with the occasional rumbling of a truck far below, keeps me from forgetting how close I am to town. When it comes, the nightmare is all sound, no sights; the inside of my head stays darker than the inside of my tent. Voices, aggressive male voices, just outside my tent, clumsy footsteps coming close enough to tread on the thin tentwall, sounds of rough, powerful hands beginning to pull the entrance flaps apart—I wake up to my own voice shouting "NO!" Then I drift off to sleep again, lulled by the now faint coyote music.

Like me, the coyotes are Western transplants who've found their way to the forests of the Northeast. The original New England large predators had been hunted to extirpation by the mid-nineteenth century: the last wolf was shot in 1850 and the last mountain lion in 1858, in Emily Dickinson's Amherst, though big cats hung on in Maine till the early 1890s. Habitat loss did at least as much as bounty hunting to drive them out. As I walk past the old stone fences and foundation stones of a lost farming culture, I'm reminded that by 1845, the year Thoreau went to live "alone, in the woods" at Walden Pond, over 80% of Massachusetts had been deforested. With the wolves and pumas went the beavers, the wild turkeys, most of the white-tailed dear, and virtually all the black bears, with just a hundred or so holed up in the deep woods by 1970.

Fortunately for the wildlife, about a century earlier, legions of farmers had already begun abandoning the hard life and rocky soil of what was once the North Woods in favor of burgeoning industries and the soft, fecund soil of the Midwestern plains. (Visiting South Bend one spring, I remember feeling almost giddy from the waves of rich humus scent wafting from freshly turned Indiana soil the color of dark chocolate cake.) Left fallow, thousands of abandoned farms grew over with white pines, which were in turn clearcut during the logging boom of the early twentieth century. The third generation forest, at last, was left more or less in peace, covering the New England hills once more but now with a mix of deciduous hardwoods, dominating over the remaining pines and hemlocks at lower elevations, and with the resurgent spruce and fir forest higher up.

Backpacking the trails of Massachusetts, I learn to identify any number of hardwoods—red maples, sugar maples, and, for some reason my favorite, the slender, broad-leaved goosefoot maples; beeches, with their elephant skin bark, and the silver, yellow, and paper birches; white oaks and mountain ash;

pin cherry and quaking aspen. I'm encouraged to find how many hemlocks, especially further north, still look free of the wooly adelgid infestation that's killed off the hemlocks bordering my yard at home, its telltale sign a sickly white encrustation that reminds me of the fake snow on a PVC Christmas tree.

The third-generation woods I hike through show little evidence, apart from those ghostly, decrepit stone walls and the odd long-forsaken apple tree, of any history of homesteading and deforestation. In the mild, but not yet cool, autumn light, with the leaf change in full swing, I make an amazing discovery: the real beauty of a New England fall has as much to do with light as with leaves. As I hike through the Berkshire Hills around Dalton, heading for a night at Crystal Mountain campsite, the path again runs half-hidden under leaffall, though plenty of leaves—yellow-green, yellow, and russet—still cling to the trees overhead. They warm the soft light as it passes through and then radiates back up from the yellow leaves underfoot. I find myself walking through an almost palpable glow, bathed in light the color and, to look at it, the texture of wildflower honey, a light I'm tempted to call unearthly—but I know better.

Most of the Colonial-era forest critters have returned along with the trees and by now built up healthy populations: in my section hiking years I'll see the wild turkey transition from a rare backwoods sighting to a common suburban distraction. We still dream of the return of the big cats, though I meet several people hiking the Trail who swear that someone they know and trust swears to an unambiguous puma sighting somewhere in New England. The wolves, though, may have been permanently boxed out by the coyotes, who have taken not only their ecological niche but some of their DNA, interbreeding with red wolves on their long eastward trek through Canada. I've read that Eastern coyotes can boast as much as one quarter wolf ancestry. That long night in the Shaker campsite, I'm certain I hear the wolf blood in their howling.

Despite two waves of deforestation, you can still find a few remnants of the ancient forest. Two weeks later, I follow the Trail south up the Jug End, gaining a thousand feet in the first mile from the road. The bracing climb is (as always) more than worth it. From the top, under the high cloud cover, I can see the Greylock massif dominating the northern horizon and the sweet pastures and farmland below. Heading south, I get my first taste of the Taconics, uncouth southwestern neighbors to the Berkshires that ought to be just as well known. The trail follows a sharp ridge of quartz-veined schist almost to the Connecticut border, surprisingly rugged given the low elevations, a foretaste for northbound hikers of the White Mountains to come. After a sharp descent from Mount Everett, the high point at just 2600 feet, the ridge trail climbs again through dense thickets of mountain laurel, which I promise myself to revisit in May, when the evergreen shrubs will be in bloom. Wide views open to the east over a series of sharp drop-offs, acres of green fields and a river valley and, further south, a slate blue lake. Vultures soar on the air currents not far overhead. At the top of Mt. Race I again encounter krumholz, but of an unusual sort, dwarf pitch pine rather than spruce or fir, twisted by the wind into charmingly grotesque forms straight out of a German fairy tale.

After a long, gentle descent the trail leaves the ridge to bottom out at Sawmill Brook, which I cross on a series of broad, flat rocks, the last few filmed with half an inch of flowing water. Now the trail hooks west with the brook into Sages Ravine. There's something mysterious and electric about this spot that I can't put my finger on, but that deepens with every step. Maybe it's the way the powerful stream gushes around and between and then cascades over the boulders that rise everywhere along its bed, or the way the woods on the far side look inviting and a little forbidding at the same time. Maybe it's the huge hemlocks that now start to tower over both banks, the tallest I've ever seen in the East. They give the ravine a forest primeval effect, and for good reason—I later discover that I've hiked through one of the very few stands of ancient forest left in Massachusetts.

I set up in a large, primitive-style campsite (no shelter, no fires), cook dinner on my tiny Primus stove under the hemlocks, and sleep deeply as a light rain patters harmlessly and rolls off the tautly guyed tent fly. The morning is all mist, rocks, trees, and stream sounds and the ravine looks even more enchanted than the afternoon before: I feel that I've somehow slipped inside a ninth-century Chinese scroll painting. Although I know the ravine is most likely named after a local family, I can't help thinking of this as the spiritual abode of T'ang dynasty mountain sages, a feeling that recurs during many return visits over the years to come.

September-October 2006. I finish backpacking the Trail in Massachusetts over the fall of 2005. In September, camping out a few miles north of Cheshire, leaves fall on and around my tent all night with soft rustles; at midnight, a barred owl calls from somewhere in the forest. In November, hiking north to October Mountain, needle ice pushes up from the frozen soil like fragile crystal stalks. In early December, I backpack from the Housatonic to just north of Lake Buel, a last connect-the-dots hike between the endpoints of earlier trips, and backtrack to sleep again at Tom Leonard shelter above the Ice Gulch in the East Mountain forest. A frigid but lovely, lonesome hike: in two days I see no one, picking out the trail under a thin snow cover, and in the early dark I build a fire of fallen branches against the cold. The temperature drops to 15 degrees and I reluctantly dive into my down bag, the stars blazing in the chilled air. By morning my water bottles have frozen solid and the clouds have returned. I hike out in a steady, light snow.

Another September and it's time to cover as much of Vermont as I can in the cool fall weekends. One Friday on the cusp of October I teach my 1 p.m. class in hiking clothes, end it a little early, and literally run to my car. If I push every speed limit and stay just ahead of the early rush hour, I can make it to the trailhead near Bennington with barely enough daylight for the short hike south to Congdon Shelter. Then I'll be set up for a long Saturday, hiking back past my car to climb Glastonbury Mountain and sleep at the Goddard shelter, just off the AT and a little short of the summit.

With Halloween a month away, one of the Trail magazines I get in exchange for annual support comes out with a feature on the spooky history of the Bennington Triangle, only a few days before my hike. Most of it is just silly: a Bigfoot-like creature, UFO's, strange lights among the trees. But some of the claims sound more legitimately weird, like the way people's dogs would disappear in the area of Hell Hollow Brook. And not just dogs. From 1945 to 1950, five different people simply vanished in the woods or on the highway where I plan to leave my car. An experienced outdoor sportsman, a Bennington College student off for a day hike, an old guy on a bus who never reached the Bennington stop, an eight-year-old boy playing near the highway, a middle-aged woman not far from her campsite—the only one whose body was ever found, in an area searchers had poured over months earlier.

So of course I share this information with my teenage kids, leaving out the part about the little boy. Lida, at eleven, has developed an utterly rationalistic view of the world combined with a keen taste for all things folkloric and paranormal, in a "wouldn't it be cool if that were true" spirit—somewhat like her Dad. She shivers, laughs, and makes me promise to take pictures. Nate, a few days from turning fourteen, finds the disappearances much more ominous and almost certainly the work of a mastermind serial killer, so I do the math with him: assuming the killer was at least around twenty at the time of the first disappearance, I'd be dealing with a reassuringly decrepit eighty year old, and one who had not struck for more than half a century. "But his *son* would be the perfect age!," Nate counters—an unsettling thought in more ways than one.

So when I leave my car on VT9 with under two hours of daylight to cover more than four miles and climb a thousand feet, I half expect to feel a few shivers of my own. (Appropriately enough, the class I taught in my long sleeve zip-T was on the Gothic novel.) Leaving one of my water bottles and most of my food in the car, I hike quickly despite the elevation gain. The skies have begun to darken by the time I've gone half a mile, and the thickened light dapples through the tree cover, the leaves taking on color—yellows and red—but with few as yet on the damp ground. The trail is easy to follow and the woods feel more softly inviting than sinister. By the time I near the campsite, fifteen minutes ahead of the dark, a waxing gibbous moon has come out and adds its own pale gleam to the pleasant, dusky light. The campsite is dark and deserted—a perfect horror movie set up. I unpack quickly in the empty lean-to, a kid's playhouse of a shelter, with twin bunks on each side, a picnic table squeezed in between, and, unexpectedly, some windows, one on each of the three walls (the entire front is, as usual, open to the weather). I place my candle-lantern on the picnic table and eat the dinner sandwich I've brought from home. The stream nearby is running high with the rains from earlier in the day, its constant gurgling penetrating the shelter as it churns over its bed of rocks. I feel as peaceful as I've ever felt sleeping outdoors, and I can't find room in myself for even a sliver of apprehension. I'm just too happy to be alone with a full heart in the fall woods on such a night. Or not quite alone—I share the lean-to with an inquisitive but harmless mouse.

The next day's hike proves just as insistently pleasant. The day starts out bright and cool, just warm enough to hike in a T-shirt (without the backpack I'd need to put on my fleece). The trail has dried out a little, but stays fairly muddy at the lower elevations—this is Vermont, the mud state, after all. I'm grateful for all the bog bridges, sometimes planks, sometimes split logs, that generations of volunteers have built and maintained. I take my time, enjoying the cool air, the leaves, the gradual ups and downs, maybe 2500 feet in all. It's hard to find anything sinister to photograph for Lida—I settle for a twisted snag of a dead tree and a looming granite crag, but really the most honest descriptor for this section of trail would be the disappointingly tame "pretty." Hell Hollow Brook itself turns out to be a more docile cousin of last night's shelter stream, clear and sparking in the mid-day sun, easy to cross on a series of rounded stones. Perhaps there's a vortex somewhere downstream that could suck in large dogs without a trace, but here a terrier could amble across with nothing more serious than wet paws. Near the top of Glastenbury Mountain, at the epicenter of the spooky Bennington Triangle, I can't find anything more uncanny than a gnarly looking log, and I haven't seen a soul, disembodied or not, all day.

Until, a short walk from the summit, the shelter comes into view a little to the west. Not so much the shelter itself as the solitary figure standing near it, square shouldered and ramrod straight. There's something off about him—for one thing, he's dressed in black; his hiking clothes look more like paramilitary fatigues, the kind you would associate with SWAT teams or Central American death squads. Between the clothes and the military bearing, I can't help scanning for a weapon of some sort, a long knife holstered on his thigh or maybe even a sidearm, but I see nothing more threatening than what look from here like combat boots. There's something else, though, that feels off-putting but that I can't bring into focus until I get still closer. As I approach the shelter the man in black regards me coolly with one hawk-like eye; where the other should be, there's an empty socket.

The kids will be so happy.

I do what you always do in any even slightly dubious backwoods encounter, starting a conversation to see what kind of vibes I get, what kind of sensations register in my gut as we talk. It's only four p.m. so I can always keep going if something feels wrong, though I've put in fourteen and a half miles and would just as soon call it a day. We exchange trail names—I'm going by Cascader, in tribute to my Washington State roots, he's "Just Jim"—and starting points—Jim has come south as I've hiked north. I then ask him if anyone else so far is staying at the shelter.

"There were some others," he says, reflectively; adding, after a pregnant pause, "but they're gone now."

Better and better. There's another shelter four miles north, if I don't mysteriously vanish first.

We keep talking, though, and it appears that ol' Jim thruhiked some years back, served in Viet Nam (that explains the missing eye and martial bearing), worked for years as a Boston housing cop (which accounts, I suppose, for his taste in hiking clothes). We chat for another hour as a trail-battered distance hiker shows up and then, just ahead of a rain storm, a young couple out for the weekend with their golden retriever (who appears unscathed by the Hell Hollow Brook crossing). We cook our dinners together under the shelter's generous overhang (an all too rare feature). I tell everybody about the Bennington Triangle mysteries to much amusement all round.

The kids too laugh when I tell them the story of my comically unspooky and undramatic hike. They've never seriously doubted that Dad would come back in one piece as always. They've picked up on my total lack of anxiety about spending time in the woods alone, and they've each spent enough time outdoors with me to know that the mountains feel (and are) a lot safer than the city. There's something else, though, that really would keep them up nights if we told them. Some time before Halloween I'll move out—I already have a rented apartment waiting for me a few miles away and I've started a stockpile hidden in the back of the garage for things I'll need to make it livable. We'll wait until a couple of weeks after Nate's birthday to break the news but, at this point, my wife is no less eager for me to leave than I am. I'll keep coming back safely from my hikes, but it won't be to the place that, for a few more weeks, we all still call home.

November 2006. If the skies stay clear I'll see shooting stars tonight. A short but intense Leonid meteor shower is scheduled for November 18 and I'm heading for a front row seat, back on Glastenbury Mountain, far from any ambient light. This time I start twelve and a half miles to the north of Goddard, getting up by six a.m. in order to reach the trailhead on the Arlington –West Wardsboro Road by ten. Once more I see no one on the trail, no people, that is, because there are plenty of other creatures to say hello to: a red squirrel, some chipmunks, blue jays, ravens, and lots of slate-gray juncos flitting about. Steadily gaining elevation through a beech forest, dotted with knots of hemlocks and, higher up, some firs, I scare up a pair of grouse after hearing one drumming on the side of the trail, a sound that at first I mistake for a sudden quick throbbing in my own ears. Despite climbing almost the whole way I hike fast, energized by the cool air, excited to be back in the hills.

This is the first chance I've had to return to Vermont for another weekend hike—moving, setting up the apartment, laying the groundwork for a different life has taken up nearly all my time. The new place is cheap (it's in the less prosperous town next door, across from a Kentucky Fried Chicken franchise) but surprisingly roomy. There's a big loft where I can inflate an aerobed and unroll an old futon when the kids come for the stipulated weekends, or use as a meditation room, an old habit I've just returned to, when I'm alone. It also has a study where I can write and a funky downstairs living room that I rarely use except when the kids are over. In a year or so I'll buy a condo in a nicer part of the same town, just a five-minute drive from the old house, but for now this is working.

I reach the Glastenbury summit about an hour before the sun sets, around 4:30 today, so there's plenty of time to climb the old fire tower on top. At 3748 feet, plenty tall by Southern New England standards, Glastenbury gives views in all directions, at least once you've climbed the tower to look out over the trees. Stratton Mountain, with a fire tower of its own, looms up to the east and north. All around, you can see low, densely forested mountains, the Greens, the Taconics, even Greylock in Massachusetts. The air chills—it's not much above freezing now that the sun's so low—and I make the short descent to the shelter. This time, no one's there to greet me and trade trailnames. By 5:45 no one else has arrived, as the woods grow completely dark.

Except for the stars. More and more and more appear as I watch the skies, perched on the edge of the shelter, bright as I've ever seen them. It's as though the stars are determined to put on a good show before they start falling to the earth. Soon the Milky Way appears, never seen from the city, a swathe of stardust across the sky, literally nebulous. Just warm enough in my down vest, balaclava, and hiking gloves, I let my mind and eyes relax and effortlessly scan, catlike, for the first shooting stars.

Five years earlier I'd taken Nate and Lida up to the roofdeck of our Cape Cod rental, on Lieutenant Island, with just a handful of widely spaced houses abutting a wildlife refuge, the night skies almost as dark as they are tonight. It was their first sight of the Milky Way. At first they could hardly believe their eyes. It was a week of beautiful weather and we went up night after night to starwatch. The next summer we brought a start chart and learned to name the brightest summer stars: Altair, Vega, Arcturus. We would trace out Draco and Cassiopeia and, nearby, Ursa Major and Minor, trusty pointers to Polaris, the North Star, at the end of the Little Dipper's handle. So they would never feel lost in the woods at night.

Clouds begin to streak in from below the southern horizon two hours before the meteors are scheduled to start raining down. I will them to drift away again, but the atmosphere grows misty and then completely opaque, so I slide into my bag, sleeping in boxers and long-sleeved zip-T, leaving the balaclava on for added warmth. We must have made four or five Lieutenant Island trips in all, rare weeks of untroubled happiness in a marriage that seemed to run on conflict, for reasons I could not understand any more than I could change them. I watched myself grow defensive and bitter, often drinking myself into numbness once the kids were in bed. Finally I couldn't bear them thinking that this was what a marriage should be. Or that this was what a man should be.

The return to backpacking after almost thirty years was part of a program, I'm now coming to see, to reclaim some version of who I'd set out to be in my late teens. I knew that what I was seeking was still there, the way you know the stars are still there on a cloudy night, the way you know the Milky Way is still there though you haven't seen it for years or maybe decades through the artificial glare. Every weekend in the woods brought me back in touch with something I couldn't name and couldn't fail to recognize, like a place I'd long lost sight of but never forgotten. After two years of hiking the Trail whenever I could get away, I knew it was time to start changing the conditions of my life.

I fall asleep at 8 p.m. and wake up ten hours later, hiking back to the car as a few tentative snowflakes fall through the bare branches, settling on muddy ground grown stiff with the cold. Winter looks to be coming early, but I'm determined to get another weekend in before the end of the year. Again I see no one on the trail, but I meet a nice local guy in the parking area, a veteran hiker about my age, who gives me some tips on snowshoe backpacking.

Two weeks later I leave the same trailhead to hike north past Stratton Pond to a shelter just inside the Lye Brook Wilderness. The end of November brought a freakish warm spell to New England—in Boston we get some 68 degree days—but for the past twenty-four hours high winds from the north have pulled in new weather system, cold and wet. By the time I reach Vermont the rains tail off though the winds keep gusting, 40 miles an hour or more; climbing Stratton Mountain occasional snow flurries send flakes dancing wildly around me. Aside from a pair of hunters I meet at the parking area, who arrive on top of Stratton just in time to snap my picture next to the fire tower before they disappear into the woods, again I encounter no one for two days.

Just past the summit, starting the long descent toward Stratton Pond, I'm stopped in my tracks by something I've never seen before and never expected to see. The patch of earth between two thick roots of a tall fir tree is moving, rhythmically heaving up and down. My first wild thought is that some large animal has burrowed just beneath the surface and is now laboring to breathe underground. This thought passes instantly but I remain standing still, amazed and perplexed, watching the ground rise and fall, rise and fall. With the rapidly cooling temperatures the damp earth has half frozen—ascending the mountain I step over needle ice to avoid crushing the frost blooms under my boots—and the heaving winds have found a hidden passageway under the tree's elaborate root system where the soil has washed out. With each gust the frozen layer of ground lifts and then subsides. Again I think of a line from Coleridge's dream poem, *Kubla Khan*: "As if this earth in fast thick pants were breathing." But this "miracle of rare device," like the summer ice caves I visited a hundred miles south, is no dream.

In just a few miles the trail takes a bend around the shore of Stratton Pond, an ordinary miracle: wooded, secluded, clear, dug out of the rock by retreating glaciers over 10,000 years ago. A narrow trail branches off to the left that according to my map leads to a shoreline campsite hidden from view, and I decide to come back and sleep there some night. For now, instead, I keep to the AT for another five miles until the Branch Pond Trail appears, leading a half mile into the Lye Brook Wilderness to yet another thoughtfully designed, recently rebuilt shelter. The cold has kept me moving along briskly and I reach Douglas Shelter at three in the afternoon, but with not much more than an hour to go before the early sunset.

Alone in the shelter, I let my air pad fill but leave my sleeping bag in its stuff sack for now, using it as a meditation cushion as I sit for half an hour facing the open front, my gaze lightly focused on nothing in particular. By December the North Woods have gotten remarkably quiet. No birds sing this afternoon, no creature disturbs the fallen leaves, the winds have died down and the trees stand calm and unruffled. I take in the silence; I let the silence take me in.

Then I jump into action, gathering brush for the fire that will give me an extra few hours of light. Two weeks ago, working with wet sticks, I failed to get a campfire going, a painfully embarrassing admission for someone who grew up backpacking in rainsoaked Washington State. So this time I go all out. I place a large square of highly flammable birch bark over the damp ash in the firepit, peeling off thin strips from a smaller piece to use as tinder: they curl themselves up and leave lots of air for quick combustion. Around and over this I gently place dead fir twigs, borrowed from near the trunk of a dying tree and protected from rain by the still green needles above them—the desiccated evergreen sap acts as a natural accelerant. Over that I build a loose teepee of the slenderest, driest twigs I can find, girdled around by a rising square tower of kindling sticks, with larger sticks near at hand to place at diagonals across the tower when the time comes and with more dead fir sprigs for emergency boosting as needed. Then a graded series of thicker branches, boot-snapped into appropriate lengths, to add around and over when the flames grow hot enough, with a charred log at one end of the pit to prop them up with. As a boy I was taught to build teepee fires, box ("log cabin") fires, and lean-to fires. But the best way, I've discovered, is to start with a teepee, corral it with a box, and be ready to build a lean-to over it.

Nothing can stop this fire. It crackles brightly for a good two hours as I cook dinner on my tiny stove and sip at a small Nalgene flask of bourbon, a few precious ounces of 101 proof Wild Turkey. No stars tonight, just darkness and silence and solitude. And cold: before long I slide into my three-season sleeping bag, reinforced tonight by a silk liner, and cinch the mummy hood tightly around my head. I'm just warm enough to sleep. Soon the fire's last embers have blinked out and the darkness becomes total.

September 2008. I've left my car at a trailhead just off US2 and then walked the five miles into the center of Gorham, at the north end of the White Mountains, where a shuttle will take me to Pinkham Notch. Road walking always goes fast, even with a backpack, and I've arrived early enough to get some coffee and make a call from my cellphone before shutting it off and packing it away for the weekend. So I call Dad, who's been in an assisted living place in West Seattle for the past few years, ever since I persuaded him, with great difficulty, to move there once it became painfully clear he could no longer take care of himself. Usually Dad wants to know all about my hikes, though he quickly loses track of the details, but today he only talks about himself. The conversation leaves me with a lot to sift through over the next two days.

The shuttle leaves on the late side and by the time I cross the highway from Joe Dodge Lodge I've only got a little over four hours of daylight to gain more than 3000 of some of the toughest elevation feet on the Trail and cover the six miles to Carter Notch Hut. Though it's a perfect hiking day, cool and sunny, I soon find myself pushing my limits just to get up the first, steep 2000 feet to the Wildcat Ridge. Scrambling up jagged rock, nearly losing my balance and pitching myself down the mountainside when I stumble along a narrow, dizzying shelf, the five quick miles this morning now catch up with me. This is the kind of trail I love, rugged, primitive, uncompromising, and on top of my anxiety about beating the sunset I feel upset at not having an extra hour to pace myself and really enjoy this beautiful fall afternoon. And at moments I do, moments when I'm not fighting the mountain but dancing a wild dance with it, taking in the partial, flitting views of the equally rugged Carters, which I'll climb the next day, feeling the energy of the rockscape and of my body traversing it.

Finally I come to the north end of the Wildcat Ridge, summiting the peak called simply Wildcat A, and look down into the Carter Notch where the AMC hut appears directly below me, at the bottom of a sharp descent of over a thousand vertical feet. Now I can relax a little as I negotiate the rocky way down, and in the waning light I remember past trips here with the kids. One October weekend, picked out with sheer luck at what turned out to be peak leaf change, looking out from the top of Mt. Hight (just across the Notch) with Nate and Lida, taking in a fall foliage spectacular that you could never experience without climbing up into the heart of the White Mountains. I can still see the bands of color on the hills and peaks in every direction, a day never to be repeated and burned forever into memory. Nearing the hut and the small, tarn-like Carter Lakes, I think back to a February weekend, snowshoeing to spend the night here with Nate, his friend Willy, and Willy's dad Ron, the lakes that now reflect back a reddening sky then completely iced over. We'd shut ourselves up into the bunkroom not ten minutes before a snowstorm wilder than any I'd ever encountered came zooming out of the northeast, a thick cloud of horizontal snow flying more than falling, whirling and eddying with the pounding winds, the wood structure groaning and the roof outright howling. And then our amazement twenty minutes later when the door heaved open and in came a small band of winter hikers, brushing off snow, somehow having found their way through total white-out conditions.

That night the hut was nearly empty; tonight it's over half full but already running off-season, which means packing in all your own bedding and food, the way I prefer it. I get hot water from a large urn and pour it into my resealable pouch of tasty Mountain House beef stew, while others use the huge stove to prepare elaborate meals of pasta and sauce, steak tips and fried potatoes, spreading out cheese and crackers and opening boxes of wine. (I've come equipped with a half-liter Nalgene filled with Big House Red, a cheap and hearty California blend that pairs well with freeze dried stew.) I keep to myself and start to go over the morning's conversation with Dad, but I'm too tired to think very clearly. Tomorrow I'll need to cover fifteen miles, much of it nearly as rugged as the six I just did, over Carter Dome, Mount Hight, the Carters (South, Middle, and North), Moriah, and Middle Moriah before finally descending to the Rattle River. So I give away half my wine and go to bed early.

And get up early, the first into the kitchen at 6 a.m., boiling water in a kettle for coffee and instant oatmeal—the caretaker is still asleep and the big urn has gone cold. On the trail by seven, a pretty morning, just a few clouds in the sky, nice and cool as I climb some 1500 feet to the top of Carter Dome. Clouds continue to drift in though Mount Hight still offers an expansive view, this time the forests just streaked here and there with yellow and a few dots of early red. Once on the ridge, the downs start to feel harder than the ups and I have to scramble at times to keep from sliding down the steep granite slabs. My thighs have begun to ache but I keep going fast as I can. Between South and Middle Carter, a male spruce grouse or "fool hen," with its black and white barred breast and bright red eye markings, stands unwarily by the side of the trail, not a foot away from my striding boots. Not long after, coming up Moriah, I pass a female spruce grouse with four full-grown chicks, all of them plain brown versions of the showy male: they carelessly amble away into a thicket of dwarf evergreens.

By the time I'm negotiating the stretches of bare rock near the Moriah summit the clouds are no longer overhead—I'm inside them. The fog is humid, cool, and quite thick—I can see at most two cairns ahead of me and then nothing, no longer sure I'm even on the trail. Another hiker appears out of the mist, a Japanese woman about my age, and we confer over a puzzling hook in the trail before moving off in opposite directions. I'm on a footworn path but I'm not certain whether it's the right one or not, until I come to a trail sign and realize I've stayed on the AT but missed the short side trail to Moriah's summit, just a short scramble. Rather than turn around, I decide to climb Moriah another weekend—if anything, I'm glad to have an excuse to come back before long.

I hike my way down out of the cloud and as the mist dissipates so does any sense of rush. The trail now descends more gradually, down to the Rattle River, which it will skirt all the way back to where I left my car. My mind drifts away from the hike and I start planning a phone call to my sister Lisa in Seattle, wondering how much exactly to pass along to her from a conversation that Dad, of course, has told me to keep between the two of us. But I'm too disturbed by it, by the notes of anguish and even desperation in his voice.

Dad began to fail noticeably, mentally as well as physically, by his late 70s, and when Mom died and left him on his own at 81, he could just get by with someone coming in to help a few days a week. Less than two years later, just before Christmas, he fell and ruptured three discs in his back. I arrived in time to help transfer him to a rehab, nursing, and eldercare facility that the ambulance driver assured us was "the very best place like this in all Seattle." Lisa worked some magic to get Dad the option for the one available assisted living apartment. My job was to get Dad to agree to move into it. That turned out to be the hardest thing I'd ever done, not least because some part of me really did not want to treat my father the way I treated my children, telling him what he could and couldn't do. For almost two weeks I projected breezy certainty while wrestling with all kinds of inner doubt. It felt as though my own childhood, that hidden remnant of it that still needed Dad to be the dad, was coming to an end. Both of my Seattle sisters along with half the nursing staff came down with norovirus, as did Dad himself. So I took over most of his physical care, reviving old skills from a stint as a nursing home orderly decades before. Dad and I grew incredibly close over that time and I also, often, felt incredibly alone.

After I got back to Boston and let him know I'd arrived safely, I let a long time go by without calling, well over a month. My sisters had nothing disturbing to report but I still worried that Dad might feel I'd betrayed him, might yell at me when I called or worse. I didn't want him to tell me I'd let him down, tricked or pressured him into leaving the only home he'd known for more than half a century. I might not need his approval any more, those days seemed to be past, but I still needed him to love me.

When I finally called him to ask how he was settling in, he answered in a voice I can only call beaming, "Al, it's just like high school!" Coming from Dad, senior class president, valedictorian, star of the school Gilbert and Sullivan musicals, this could only be good. Naturally gregarious but socially isolated for years, he had suddenly found himself again voted most popular, with a steady group of male friends and a blue-rinsed bevy of female admirers. Until one of them, literally the girl next door (on his third floor hallway), managed to get him all to herself. Which is where the trouble started.

Truly enamored, I believed, but extremely possessive, Dad's girlfriend began forbidding him to talk to most other women, monitored his visitors, and sometimes even screened his calls. I came to wonder if her jealous behavior was made worse by some mild dementia of her own, though in general she used her relatively intact cognitive skills to dominate my father: genial, charming even, but easily confused. She blatantly tried to put some distance between him and us, his kids. All this, of course, troubled me, but Dad seemed so happy. Until she began pressing him, forcefully and relentlessly, to marry her. That's what the call had been about. Dad wanted things to stay the way they were, but he felt trapped. He told me she was making him miserable, that he even felt physically ill a lot of the time, but he couldn't just end the relationship. "The sex, Al, I can't do without the sex." More than I'd ever wanted to know.

Hiking out along a stream, especially in decent weather and down a graded decline, counts as one of the pure pleasures of backpacking. The brook sounds, the rustling of birds and scurrying of animals drawn to the water, the little cascades and occasional pools, the mossy banks and, today, the first few leaves falling into the water and skimming along on the current. I feel strong and happy. I really shouldn't have been able to manage such a rugged twenty-one mile stretch over a day and a half, not to mention the five-mile road walk the first morning. Especially seeing that for various reasons I hadn't been out on the trail for almost half a year, since early April. But I take the last two miles fast, carried along by physical momentum. (The next day both my thighs will burst into fire with every footstep.)

Just past the Rattle River shelter, sited much too close to the highway for my liking, I see a curious, almost fantastical little creature, mouse-like but with an extra long tail, hind legs bent back almost like a jack-rabbit's, and hopping to the side of the trail like a tiny kangaroo. A meadow jumping mouse, the only one I have ever seen. It gives me a moment of pure joy. I drive home, work out a way with Lisa to deal with Dad's problem, fly to Seattle to help get it in place, and by the time I return for Christmas, everything has settled down nicely. And when we take Dad out for dinner, I don't hesitate to order for him.

October 2008. Leaving Rattle River and the outskirts of Gorham, the Trail heads north across the big Androscoggin River and then climbs doggedly, almost 1800 feet, up Mount Hayes. The Androscoggin Valley marks the end of the White Mountains and the beginning of the Mahoosucs, which extend well into Maine, though today my twelve miles will land me just south of the state border. The Mahoosucs are one of the wildest, most rugged, and most remote feeling sections of the AT, a country of sphagnum bogs and stunted evergreens, jagged rock and glacial ponds. The occasional woods road rarely comes more than within a few miles of the trail: no road crosses it for thirty miles. The Androscoggin also marks about as far as I want to drive for a weekend backpack. I've now covered all but a few miles of the Appalachian Trail from northern Connecticut to here just short of Maine, following the series of mountain groups tributary to the great Appalachian chain as it stretches north through New England: the Taconics, the Berkshires, the Green Mountains and the Whites. For the next six years, my autumn overnights will mostly take me to various New Hampshire "4Ks," the forty-eight peaks over 4000 feet in height (only a third of which lie directly on the AT). I'll do this to stay in hiking shape, to range more widely in the White Mountains, and, mostly, to have an excuse to keep hiking in the bracing fall weather I love.

Today I stay just warm enough in shorts, T-shirt, hat, and hiking gloves, thanks to the backpack and the elevation gain (about 3000 feet in all by the time I get to Gentian Pond). It will take me seven hours to cover (to be precise) 11.8 miles, and a fine seven hours it is. Just a few miles out of Gorham and I'm well into one of the least tamed and most varied sections of the AT. Streams flow across the trail and then cascade down below it, one running out of Page Pond, just to the left, one draining into Dream Lake, just to the right—moose tracks crisscross the trail and the muddy areas below it. Narrow bog bridges, demanding extra balance, alternate with wooded stretches (beech, birch, and elm mixing with the firs and spruces), which in turn lead to higher ridge walks on rough granite and sparkly schist. The leaf change is well underway this far north and layers of gold-brown leaves cover and sometimes hide the footpath: several times I need to backtrack after losing the trail. Some more brightly colored leaves yet cling to the trees overhead, filtering the light which now once more bounces up from the forest floor as a luminous glow, but brighter and more rarified than the honey-like autumn light I remember hiking through in Massachusetts. Though never rising above 3000 feet, in the highest spots the trail leaves the forest behind and only mosses and lichens grow among the rocks, giving the bare summits an alpine feel.

I pass deer as well as moose tracks, but spot no animal larger than the ruffed grouse I startle from the trail, closely followed by two more. Shortly afterwards, I nearly go flying off the trail myself as I step right into a shallow rill, gliding over mossy rock and completely hidden by fallen leaves, but a desperate thrust with my carbide-tipped hiking staff keeps me on my feet. I arrive at Gentian Pond around 5:30 with half an hour of daylight to spare, feeling that delicious combination of tiredness and humming physical energy one gets after a good day of strenuous backpacking.

The big shelter is empty—once again I've seen no one on the trail all day—and the bunk area looks inviting, but I came determined to tent tonight so I set up quickly as shadows start to lengthen from the rocky peaks that rim the pond. I cook dinner at the fire ring but tonight I don't feel like building a fire, so I break out my little candle lantern to have some flickering light nearby as the dusk gradually deepens to a clear, dark night. I read for a while in my tent and come out at 8:30 to see the sky again blazing with stars, looking infinitely deep tonight, the Milky Way as broad and bright as it's ever been. Stream sounds come to me from somewhere near the pond. Though the winds stay low, the temperature quickly drops below freezing, sending me back to the warmth of my tent and sleeping bag. In the middle of the night I wake to hear something, probably a deer, running by just a couple of feet from my tent. Then I fall back to sleep until early in the morning, when a solitary loon calls out eerily and unmistakably from the water.

By the time I look out at the pond the loon has flown off, but I have otherwise good luck with birdspotting as I hike back towards town. I see both blue jays and gray jays—these last known as "camp robbers." Once on a dayhike in the Whites, with my family and a family of friends, a gray jay kept flitting about us on a snack break as I sternly warned all the kids not to feed it. Suddenly it swooped down, stuck its needle-sharp claws through my T-shirt and into my chest, and bit off a third of the Cliff bar I was eating. Nate and Lida couldn't stop giggling. (I couldn't blame them.) Further down the trail, my eyes are caught by an unusual woodpecker climbing an oak tree—the size of a hairy woodpecker, but with zebra stripes running down its back. It can only be a northern three-toed, a rare sighting, one for the life list if I bothered to keep one. Finally, on the way back down Mount Hayes, I happen upon a barred owl, still out in the late morning sun. It perches on a tree rooted on the mountainside below the trail, so that the two of us wind up at eye-level as I stop to regard it. The owl sits with its back to me, but it turns its head an impossible 180 degrees to look directly at me. Once, twice, three times it rotates its head to gaze at me, not glancingly but long and hard, as though trying to read my soul. And then, with no apparent effort, it lifts off and flies, noiselessly, deeper into the woods.

SPRING

To carry yourself forward and experience myriad things is delusion.
That myriad things come forth and experience themselves is awakening.

Dōgen Kigen, *Genjō Kōan*

March 2005. When Lida and I get out of the car we find up to a foot of snow still on the ground. The Boston area has long thawed out and the roads have been clear the whole way; spring officially began a week ago. But in Western Massachusetts winter clings. I ask Lida if she wants to turn around and drive home, but she has her heart set on this hike: her first "real" backpacking trip, since the hikes we've taken up to the AMC huts in the White Mountains don't involve sleeping or cooking out of doors. We're both wearing full cut leather boots and I've brought a Leki staff for each of us, so it's not exactly crazy to go ahead, especially since a sole hiker has recently broken out the trail. So we shoulder our backpacks and start our five-mile walk through snowy woods to October Mountain.

The threatened rain holds off and we have some fun scrambling down an icy rock outcropping. Lida shows me where a bear has recently scratched deeply into a hemlock trunk and when we stop for lunch, apples and bread and cheese, she points out that the snow is alive with movement, small black specks ceaselessly hopping up and down. Springtails, popularly called "snow fleas," drawn out from buried leafcover by the sun that has now come out to begin melting the snow. The woods are quiet and there's no one else out today but us: today is Easter Sunday.

We hike on, Lida taking the lead now that the path has been further beaten out by several pairs of boots, until she stops short near a thicket of bushes to tell me that the trail has disappeared. The footsteps we've been following meander in a small circle and then give out where the group that made them must have given up and turned around. I can see why—there's no telltale white blaze in sight except for the one we've just passed. I hop across a brook and walk up a small rise, where I finally see a white blaze not far ahead. Now it's our turn to break trail as we ascend the small mountain.

I go ahead, trying to keep my stride short, stomping down the snow that drifts in places up to a foot and a half. It's hard going for Lida, who has to raise her legs high to stay in my steps, postholing, and I start to worry we made the wrong choice. But she toughs it out and, at last, the trail levels and the shelter comes into view, the snow around it untrodden aside from some faint coyote tracks.

We build a fire, gathering dead windfall caught in the lower branches of the trees surrounding us, lining the fire pit, half full of snow, with dead wood and then with birch bark, starting a blaze with a single match. After a freeze dried meal and some chocolate we go to bed with the early dark, claiming the high bunks on either side of the open shelter. Some time later Lida wakes me up and at first I'm disoriented, thinking it must be dawn though my watch reads 11 p.m. She's upset, afraid to wake me up and more afraid to walk into the woods alone, so I remind her I'm there to take care of her. I stop myself from adding that I always will be.

Lida heads to the privy while I stand guard. The moon, close to full, has come out while we slept, and the snow-covered woods and hills all around shine with its reflected glow, creating a ghostly version of daylight. I stand in the center of a hushed, luminous world and wait, barely breathing, my heart full, until I hear my daughter's boots crunching the snow as she returns to the shelter. Silently, we climb up to our bunks and go back to sleep, until dawn comes in earnest.

April 2006. I leave my car in the same pullout I used for my first climb up Moosilauke, this time heading south toward the Hexacuba Shelter, just over the summit of Mount Cube. Dozens of blowdowns cross the path, as the trail maintainers have not come through yet. I like this. It gives me a taste of backpacking in older days, when trails were wilder, less groomed. In addition to frequent negotiations with fallen trees, which need to be climbed over, under, or around, the large roots and slabs of rock underfoot are slick with rain that, at this temperature, could quickly gel into a sheet of glare ice. Yet I move through it all as quickly as I can, having set myself an ambitious day even apart from the obstacle course: fifteen miles and, with a series of ups and downs, over 3800 feet of elevation gain. Somehow managing to cover two miles an hour I arrive at the shelter well before sunset, scaring up a partridge and a veery along the way, dun-colored birds of early spring. Resting at the edge of the shelter I watch a wood thrush hunting in the leafrot as it approaches nearly to my feet.

Provoked by the Mount Cube's geometrical name, the shelter builders came up with a unique six-sided design for this lean-to. I take the back wall, far from the open side, a good choice when the temperature drops at night and some flecks of snow blow in. By morning the snow has become a misty rain, the temperature hovering just above freezing. My trail breakfast always includes a drink I invented early on and then stick to religiously: a packet of cocoa (the more calories the better) slit open at the top, spiked with two spoonfuls of instant espresso, and resealed with tape. This always both jolts me into full consciousness and sends me to the privy, or into the woods to dig a cathole. Not all that surprisingly, Hexacuba shelter features a signature five-sided latrine, the Pentaprivy, which stands on a high platform cut into the hillside, reached by four steep wooden steps.

No matter how careful on the trail, hikers can let their guard down in built structures: a guy who's successfully battled rainslicked rocks and low-hanging branches all day will slam his head into a shelter beam the moment he steps inside. Today that guy is me. As I sit in the privy the temperature drops again and the light mist outside turns into a freezing rain, so that when I take my first step back out onto the platform, it's as though someone has scattered dozens of tiny glass beads in front of the door. I go flying.

As I've experienced twice before in moments of acute physical danger, time slows down dramatically, my brain processing events at two or three times normal speed. I manage to entertain three distinct thoughts during a fall that must have taken all of a second and a half. First, as my feet disappear from under me and I see just how high I am off the ground, the thought forms, "this could be bad." Then, as my left hip hits the middle step, hard, and I carom horizontally through the air, I think, "this could really be bad." And finally, when my momentum is stopped by the force of my face ramming into a tree trunk, the voice in my head says, "this could really, really be bad."

I stay motionless for a long while, partly because I'm stunned, partly because I'm viscerally afraid to see what happens when I try to move. So I lie face down on the wet ground, with plenty of time to realize, first, that with the shelter a third of a mile off the Trail and few hikers out yet, it's unlikely anyone will appear if I need help. Second, that for the only time I can remember, I've neglected to leave a trip agenda with my family, so my whereabouts will be a mystery if I fail to come home. For a long minute I ponder the irony of a life cut short by a five-sided outhouse.

Then I gather up the courage to take stock. I haven't blacked out, so there's no concussion. I send a desperate message to my toes to wiggle: they do. So my neck isn't broken. In turn I manage to flex, bend, rotate, or shrug my feet, my knees, my arms and shoulders, my fingers, my head: no spine injury or broken bones that I can detect. Now I gingerly run my tongue over my teeth: all there. Finally I raise my head and locate my eyeglasses, which have bent into a V but bend back into a wearable shape. Before putting them back on, I touch my hand to my face and it comes back covered with blood. A broken nose? I'll take it.

I don't know how I will hike fifteen miles after this but it turns out not to be a problem—I even enjoy the day. When I pass a dayhiker going up I ask him if my nose looks broken. He says it does, and then asks me if it looked broken before. I realize that I don't have a good mental picture of my own nose, though I can clearly envision all four of my siblings' noses, a couple of which do indeed look broken or at least humped. He urges me stop at a local emergency room once I'm on the road, but I just want to go home, where I find that the my nose, though badly cut, is no more broken than it was before. I will never look at a wooden structure in the mountains the same way again.

May 2005. The Trail through Connecticut, rarely rising above 1500 feet, much more rustic than wild, could hardly be considered dramatic. Yet one can have adventures anywhere on the AT—as I'm discovering on this three-day trip, the first time I've made use of a shuttle, so I can double my mileage and finish up another Trail state. It's early in May and few backpackers are out yet, so I'm not surprised to find myself alone at Mount Algo campsite. Driving one state south has taken me a bit deeper into spring: the hardwoods here show bright green at the branch tips, thrushes sing from the unseen woods, and flycatchers flit in front of the empty shelter. I spend the night in my tent, enjoying the flow of cool air through the open flaps, and wake to an odd sound I have trouble placing, half bird squawk, half mammal squeak. Peeking out of my tent I see a red fox, using a series of shrill little barks to mark out its territory.

Two hours into a seventeen-mile day to Pine Swamp, I scramble up a ledge and startle a vulture from its nest. It flies just a few feet over my head, so close that I get a blast of its breath, musty, rank, unforgettable, the very stench of death. After a long walk along the Housatonic River and some more easy climbing, I arrive at the Pine Swamp Brook lean-to where, for once, I share the shelter with another hiker. A grizzled, imperturbable 67 year old, Mountain

Dog has been hiking the Trail through New York and Connecticut in sensible ten to twelve mile stretches. Happy to have someone to talk to (he too has seen virtually no one on the Trail), he tells me about a large bear he encountered one night alone at a small shelter in New York. A big male, 400 pounds, he says, the bear tried to climb into the shelter to get at his foodbag, hanging just over his head. Mountain Dog eventually scared him away by making a racket with his cooking pot. I ask him what he did next and he answers, matter-of-factly, "I went back to sleep."

Half an hour later, each of us preparing our separate meals, I look past my new friend and tell him, coolly as I can, "Mountain Dog, there's something about you bears must just like." Fifteen feet away a small male black bear, maybe 250 pounds, looks toward us with keen interest and rises up on two legs, sniffing the air now tinged with cooking smells. A bear encounter can get dicey at this time of year—there's not much food available aside from last fall's acorn mast, and young males in particular may have yet to carve out their own territory; if they grow desperate enough they can overcome their fear of humans. I grab my camera to take a couple of quick pictures, and then the two of us make enough noise for a drunken platoon, hollering and banging lids and clapping hands. The bear spins around and bolts back into the woods. Later, I lead Mountain Dog a quarter mile away from the shelter to where we hang a bearline from the highest, longest limb I can find. The bear's visit has left me thrilled in all senses of the word: delighted, keyed up, and on edge, and I lay awake half the night expecting his return, which never comes. Mountain Dog sleeps like a bear.

May 2005. Less than a minute after Ash has turned around to go back to the Roost a cottontail zips across the trail. I take it as a good omen: within the first mile of my first "long" section hike, I've seen a mammal bigger than a squirrel, something that happens on the AT less often than you might expect. Within the next half hour, before descending from Keys Gap into Harpers Ferry, I see a veery, a Swainson's thrush, and a chestnut-sided warbler with its bright yellow cap, my first glimpse of the spring warbler wave.

By mid-May and the end of final exams I can head south for longer hikes of a week or more, plunging into the heart of spring, wildflowers blooming, birdsong filling the woods, animals of all kinds out to forage, mate, or just idle in the sun. This time I've left my car with my old friends Ash and Kim in Carlisle, Pennsylvania, which happens to border a Trail town, Boiling Springs.

Then Ash and I drove to his cabin in West Virginia, which happens to lie even closer to the AT, only a few hundred yards off. Ash inherited the Roost from his parents and it remains much as it was: unheated except by a wood fire, no plumbing, reached by a badly rutted dirt and gravel road. We spent the night in sleeping bags on the screened porch, a good transition to the first full week I'll spend living in the woods since I was a teenager. I'll hike 105 miles north, back toward my car, carrying a week's worth of food and averaging fifteen miles a day. That's the plan, anyway.

The trail descends steeply to cross the Shenandoah River on a highway bridge and then bisects the town of Harpers Ferry, which I rush through, eager to get back into the hills. I stop for a break, though, at Jefferson Rock, with its view of the confluence of the Shenandoah and the Potomac, which I try in vain to imagine as Thomas Jefferson himself might have seen it, before all the steel and concrete. (He called it a view worth crossing the Atlantic for.) Then after a trudge on the flat C&O canal path, the trail finally climbs back up, 500 steep feet, to the Weverton Cliffs, with a much more countrified view of the Potomac meandering below. A couple more miles and I reach the Ed Garvey shelter. I've finished my first thirteen and a half miles early: it's only 2:30 in the afternoon.

After clambering back up from the spring, the hardest climb of the day, I check out the shelter, named for one of the first hikers to publish a book-length account of the Trail. Garvey's book makes a telling contrast with Earl Shaffer's *Walking with Spring*, which appeared later but describes the very first end-to-end hike of the AT—I've brought it with me to reread on this hike. Shaffer, one of my heroes, hiked alone, stayed in towns just long enough to resupply, mainly slept out of doors, and gave loving attention to the Trail's natural features and creatures. Garvey, instead, more or less patented the AT "thruhike" as rolling party, meeting up or staying over with a host of people he'd gotten to know over years of supporting the Trail, feasting and socializing his way north. Appropriately, the shelter named for him turns out to be the largest and most elaborate I've ever seen, with not so much a loft as a second story: if a lean-to could ever be described as palatial, this is the one. The bottom floor stays open to the elements, as usual, but the upstairs, reached by a rear ladder, features a glassed in front, two smaller windows in back, and a door that closes, a real rarity on the Trail. A phoebe has taken advantage of the large overhang over the back to build a nest where three hatchlings cheep away; every time I use the ladder she nervously flits off, returning only when I'm out of view again, while the chicks stretch their fuzzy heads out of the nest and open their beaks wide, begging me to feed them in her absence.

A few hours later, after I've had dinner, I find myself glad for the closing door as a powerful storm moves in. In between thunder blasts the high winds rattle the door and I worry for the phoebe's nest. Rain comes down hard and heavy and I think as well about the thruhiker, Bones, I met while cooking dinner in front of the shelter—when I told him he could have the whole downstairs to himself, he replied, with maybe a little more attitude than needful, "I didn't come out here to sleep in shelters." Hey, I want to counter—but don't—even old Earl Shaffer stayed in shelters. Now I just hope Bones doesn't get washed out by a storm that only gets noisier and more torrential by the hour. The temperature drops as the rain grows even harder and I cinch the hood of my mummy bag around my face.

At some point in the depths of the night I hear the door open and heavy footsteps approaching me—in the dark I can just make out three tall male forms, crowded around me, clearly meaning me harm. I try to move but I can't—I'm terrified by these men, dripping with rain, who seem born from the storm outside. Then they move off and a single female takes their place—despite the dark I can clearly see her pale face, her sad and wild expression, her long strands of wet, straggling blonde hair. She leans over me, almost protectively, and takes my hand in both of hers—her grasp is ice cold, and I struggle again to move until, finally, I manage to wake myself up. The wood plank floor around my sleeping bag is as dry as before, and I see I've been sleeping on my hand again, but it still takes me a long time to shake the feeling that all this really happened, the dream so vivid and especially the ghastly girl with her bloodless hands. I can't help wondering if the shelter is haunted. Then I shift my position and fall back asleep. It's the last nightmare I ever have on any of my hikes—the storm has blown something out of me.

I linger over breakfast but the skies refuse to clear, so I put on my raingear and head out for a twenty-mile walk in the rain. People talk about rain as though it means one thing—"How was your camping trip?" "Oh, it rained"—but I learn on the Trail that different types of rain can make for very different hikes. Some rains stay so light and tentative that seasoned hikers will stop just long enough to stretch a sylnylon cover over their backpack and leave it at that. If the rain comes on steadier but remains gentle, you can hike comfortably in a cap and rain jacket, watching the raindrops evaporate off your pants while the jacket gets damp but never wets through. In summer, rains like this can be more pleasant than a hot, bright sun—you're almost sad to see them go.

When the rain comes on heavy, you often get plenty of warning. The day starts out with clouds just edging the horizon; slowly, over a period of hours, they encroach on more and more of the sky till there's no blue left to be seen. Even then you might just get a sprinkle of five minutes or less, the big downpour still holding off. When it comes, it often comes with a brief warning: a series of rumbles high overhead, or a steady wind that suddenly comes on and lowers the temperature, or a change in the light, which both dims and takes on a strange greenish tint. That marks the time to rush underneath the thickest evergreen you can find and gear up against the storm: hat, then parka, then packcover, then, in my case, the best piece of all: the garbage bag kilt. Much lighter than rainpants, open at the bottom for maximum airflow, giving 100% protection to hiking shorts and whatever's in their pockets, and costing only a few pennies. Just slit open the bottom of a large green trashbag, tuck it all round well into your waistband, zip the rainjacket closed, and you're ready to tramp on through the storm, a low budget Braveheart.

When the rain does come, it still might surprise you by stopping short of where you happen to be walking. Traversing a ridge, you notice the sky in one direction growing fuzzy, and then you hear the rain before you see it distinctly—at first, it's hard to tell apart from wind in the trees, but as it moves near you start to hear the pattering of thousands of individual raindrops. And then, just at the ridge, it hangs: a curtain of rain so close you could almost put one hand into it, stretching parallel along the whole ridge, but keeping just to one side of you for a whole minute or even for a whole hour. If you're within a mile or two of a shelter, you can try to outrun it. At least three times I've ducked under a shelter overhang literally seconds before the deluge hit, and once I sat on the edge of a lean-to for an hour and a half while a thick wall of rain hovered not ten yards away before finally moving off.

Sometimes, though, the cloudburst comes on fast, with no warning at all. I associate these sudden tempests, when the skies can darken in moments and the temperature can drop 30 degrees in as many minutes, especially with the Green Mountains of Vermont. And the most dramatic instance of all took place, not in spring, but in fall, on the Saturday of a long Columbus Day weekend. I had reached Big Branch a little before 5 p.m., at what I had planned would be the end of a sixteen and a half mile day. But the shelter, which looked empty until I rounded a final corner, turned out to be occupied in a way I didn't like A balding, red-faced man in his mid-sixties, sprawled out on a sleeping bag, lifted his head just enough to squint at me, and then closed his eyes again. Behind him I saw along with a backpack, as expected, two large canvas shopping bags—obviously a weekend squatter and not a hiker. An attempt at conversation elicited a series of snarling replies. I wondered how many liquor bottles were in the bags. In any case, I lost all interest in staying at Big Branch—I'd taken a gamble on a shelter close to a road and lost.

Three more miles would take me to the next shelter north and if I moved quickly I would get there just before dark. So off I went, wishing the glaring old guy a pleasant evening. Fifteen minutes later the sky darkened an hour ahead of schedule—I looked up and purplish black clouds had suddenly blocked out the waning sunlight. Before I could even get my backpack off, thunder boomed overhead and a heavy rain started all at once. It was less a storm than a tempest, less a rain than a deluge. I was soaked before I could get my rain gear on and by the time I was moving again I could barely stay on the trail, between the early dark and the streaming water that quickly rose to my ankles. The lightning strikes were growing brighter and evidently closer, but I was on low ground so I didn't think much about it, until a bolt hit not ten feet ahead of me on the trail, with a simultaneous thunder clap loud enough to shake the trees. The flash was so bright and intense, lighting up the woods all around me, the strike came so suddenly, that I registered no fear—only awe and a thrill of ecstasy. There was no room for any other feeling.

Today, though, the rain soon tempers to a steady drizzle as the trail takes gentle ups and downs through the park-like Maryland woods. I hike comfortably all day—the jacket, virtually new, and the garbage bag keep the rain off while the easy terrain and cool weather mean I don't sweat too much inside the raingear: dry inside and out. After twenty miles, though, when I come to my destination, the Pogo Memorial Campsite, I find that my feet have gotten red and sore, between the wet boots and the big miles. The next day, nineteen more miles over rockier ground, takes me into Pennsylvania and leaves me with a full set of blisters, something I've never had to worry about on shorter trips. I realize I've tried to do too much too quickly, but I needed to put in two big days in order to meet my brother, Brian, at the Deer Lick campsite, which he and his young nephew can reach by a two mile hike. I find them waiting for me at one of the twin shelters and we have a great evening together, making a big campfire and breaking out a chocolate bar I've been hoarding for Shonu's benefit. Shonu, who has come from India to live with Brian and his wife, tells us this is his best camping trip ever before falling asleep. My brother and I stay up swapping stories and sipping at some bourbon, though Brian seems off to me, distracted or preoccupied. Much later I learn that, like mine, my brother's marriage is unraveling, though for now both of us are working to keep our families intact. I leave the next morning as the two of them are just waking up.

I keep the next day to a mere ten miles, belatedly giving my feet the rest they need, and reach the next campsite early enough to wash some clothes and dry them in the afternoon sun, at last shining brightly. The next day takes me through the Michaux State Forest on broad, level woodland paths, giving my feet another respite, though every step now hurts. All day I see or hear several species of birds that haunt the Trail corridor every spring: ovenbirds, a drab colored warbler smaller than a house sparrow but with a loud "TCHER" that splits the woods like a gunshot; towhees, with their unmistakable three note call, the high, last note always a little dissonant; wood thrushes and hermit thrushes, with their different and equally beautiful songs, the nightingales of the eastern forest. All ground nesters, disappearing from the suburbs thanks to habitat loss and prowling housecats. I find a phoebe nesting at nearly every shelter I visit. I take longer breaks, getting my boots off, airing my torn up feet, and stop after just thirteen miles; the next day, seventeen miles to Tagg Run shelter, will be the last full day of my week long hike.

I keep to my new hiking style, stopping every four or five miles to take off my boots, and though my feet get no better, they get no worse. The trail stays wet, but with pine trees dominating as I head north, a carpet of brown needles softens the path. I stretch the day out, not quite wanting the hike to end yet, enjoying the acres of pines, the different birdcalls, the long stretches of smooth, graded trail. The final morning, though, I speed up, eager to finish; every part of me feels great, tested and toned, aside from my bleeding feet, a problem I'm going to have to solve. By 2:30 I'm in the Boiling Springs Tavern, drinking a glass of springwater and waiting on a late lunch order of fried oysters, caesar salad, and Yuengling lager. I call Ash and tell him to hurry up and join me.

May 2006. It's a beautiful day on the North Carolina-Tennessee line, where you can walk the AT and sometimes have a foot in each state: temperatures in the 60s, a steady breeze, skies hazy on and off but no rain. I had hiked the first four miles out of Iron Mountain Gap with my friend Jim McGavran, who drove me in from his house in Charlotte and will pick me up in a week in Damascus, on the Virginia border, 102 miles north from where we started. I've known Jim for years but never been to his house or met his wife before—my conference buddy has suddenly become a real friend. Jim improvised half the evening on the piano as we drank beer and talked about my hike coming up. He finished his impromptu recital with "There's a Long, Long Trail."

Now I'm coming down into Hughes Gap and bracing for the 2000-foot climb up Roan Mountain, where I'll spend the night. Five minutes below me a paved road and a dirt pulloff come into view, along with the dozen or so bikers who have stopped there to regroup and take a break from their Harleys—the trail goes right through the burly, bearded, boisterous crew. I decide I have nothing to fear from a biker gang. They're outsiders, I'm an outsider; they're out in the elements, so am I; we're just living different versions of the great American adventure. They tease me a little once I come into view—"Hey, a hiiiiker! You want some gran-ola? You look like you need some gran-ola!"—but it's all in good spirits, and one even offers me a cold beer which I politely decline, not wanting to pack it up the mountain.

As it turns out, I have plenty of fight left in me for these last few steep miles and soon I'm nearing the summit area, covered with Catawba rhododendrons, their dark green leaves glistening in the late afternoon sun. Jim told me that morning how people will drive in from miles away to see Roan Mountain in bloom, but at this elevation, above 6000 feet, spring is still beginning and the large buds stay tightly enfolded for now. But a host of less showy wildflowers have already opened themselves to the mid-May sun, more varieties in fact than I've ever seen before. Spring beauties, with their tiny, demure pinkish-white flowers line the trail in places, and on this first day out I encounter three kinds of trillium, red, white, and painted, each with three petals set off by three matching leaves. I also pass clusters of bluets, small four petalled flowers the color of periwinkles. Later on this trip I'll encounter wild geraniums, fire pinks, Virginia bluebells, blossoming raspberry bushes, forget-me-nots, mayapples, hooded jack-in-the-pulpits, wild violets and irises, my first pink lady's slipper (a wild orchid that grows as far north as Maine) and the strange, cone-like squawroot, which does without chlorophyll and lacks any green parts—just a waxy, yellowish white. I take pictures of the flowers I don't know to identify later—which turns out to be most of them, though Jim pointed out the trilliums for me this first morning.

Roan Mountain shelter looks more like the firewarden's cabin it once was, with four walls and a door, a good thing since at 6285 feet—the highest shelter on the AT—it gets cold up here at night. But morning comes bright and sunny, as does nearly every morning of the week to come. I walk easy, covering two miles an hour, my pack a little lighter despite carrying a week's food again (I've upgraded some of my gear as lighter and better items continue to appear). My feet stay close to blister free, between the dry trails and better planning, not to mention different boots, different liner socks, and a miraculous anti-chafing balm, Bodyglide, that I reapply several times a day. I'm learning to take more breaks, against my stubborn tendency to press onward to the point of exhaustion.

Former thruhikers usually name the White Mountains as their favorite section. On this hike, though, I begin to wonder why no one seems to mention the hundred miles from Roan Mountain north. I grow more and more impressed by the sheer variety of habitats the Trail rambles through: today, for example, after the long descent through deciduous woods, the path winds over four different balds, all above 5000 feet: Round Bald, Jane Bald, Little Hump Mountain, and (big) Hump Mountain. All of these feature grassy summits bare of trees, for reasons unknown: this far south the highest Appalachians fail to rise above timberline. So a note of mystery spices the austere feel and sweeping views of these ancient, rounded peaks. In between the balds the trail weaves through pasturelands before giving way to a long, descending, rocky ravine, bursting with wildflowers. Then a mixed forest of hemlocks, laurels, beech, maple, and elm. The next day features more woods, a waterfall just off the trail, a river walk with cascades, and meadows crisscrossed by butterflies, at least five different species, black, yellow, purple, tiger striped, swallow tailed. The days stay sunny and cool, the taste of spring is everywhere.

I wake quite early the next morning to start a big day of hiking by seven. Again the Trail dazzles through sheer variety: a climb through mixed forest up White Rocks Mountain, a long descent to Dennis Cove, just past a pond and a splendidly overgrown barn, ramshackle, literally seedy, then passing through a dramatic rocky gorge, cutting deep into the earth, before arriving at spectacular Laurel Falls. Here, four thousand feet below the summit of Roan Mountain, I at last find a solitary rhododendron in bloom, as well as a pink azalea. The trail then hugs the river for a time, snaking through rocks and ledges, before the long climb, some 1800 feet, up switchbacks to Pond Flats, with no pond that I can see but a clear, gushing, pooling spring.

On a hike of any distance, you can have days when you wake up tired, when it takes hours to find your stride if you find it at all. And you can have days when you hit the trail running and you feel invincible, ready for whatever the path takes you through, surprising yourself by your pace. On days like that, a middle-aged hiker can easily fall into the illusion of renewed youth, if not agelessness, and today, climbing the switchbacks through evergreen cover, pine and rhododendron, powerfully reminded of the Cascades, I feel nineteen years old again. The illusion only grows stronger when a pair of young thruhiking brothers from the night before, Nickname and Cosmo, tall and stalwart, carrying huge staves the size of saplings, reach the spring, collapse for a bit, and share their amazement that I've gotten here so early. I go downstream from the source and soak my T-shirt in the chill water, wringing it out and putting it back on and luxuriating in the shivery feel of it on my back and chest—it will dry out again in half an hour. The brothers leave ahead of me but I catch them again as the trail bottoms out once more, at a picnic area just outside of Watauga Lake. There's a shelter coming up and, a mile beyond that, a "stealth" campsite the brothers have heard about. They invite me to come along, so we stop at the shelter for more spring water and find our way to a hidden cove just at the water's edge. I stake my tent out on a grassy bank that overhangs the lake, and the three of us go for a long afternoon swim in the cold, brackish water: we've covered nearly eighteen miles of challenging terrain and it's not yet three p.m.

The next morning I give myself a leisurely start, with only thirteen miles to cover, and I hike all thirteen slowly, once more feeling all of my fifty years. Much as I loved my shoreline berth, water lapping below me, talkative boaters passed by all night—in motorboats, canoes, rowboats, kayaks, and rafts just below my tent—waking me again and again. Without much sleep, the miles quickly catch up with me and I go from flying to crawling overnight. But the glossy evergreen shrubs, now bursting into flower, lure me on, first a single mountain laurel in bloom, then dozens if not hundreds of Catawba rhododendrons, then bright orange flame azaleas, another new flower for me and instantly one of my favorites. I drift toward sleep early, at dusk, in a skanky looking cement block shelter and jerk awake with a start as two field mice run directly at my face. But as always I've hung every scrap of food and trash and swept any crumbs out of the shelter, so the mice prowl a bit more and then leave me to sleep through an overnight thunderstorm as well as I can.

The skies clear and my energy returns for my last full day on the trail, sixteen fairly easy miles through forest and misty fields and a long ridgeline where a bustling woodcock runs across the path. Again I stay at a charmless cinderblock shelter where I linger out part of the morning, as Jim wants to hike up the trail a ways to meet me and walk me down. But Jim gets a late start and I hike faster than I'd intended, so he's just pulling into Damascus as I arrive. We spend another evening together in Charlotte and have a pointed talk about my coming divorce, as I find it impossible not to confide in him: he's wise, gentle, sometimes serious, sometimes funny, never bland. He's willing to push me hard, to make sure I'm not making a big mistake, and laying things out for him in all their stark hopelessness proves cathartic for me. On the long drive back to Boston I grow wistful, missing the trail, missing Jim.

May 2007. If I'm willing to walk another eight and a half miles I can reach the next shelter and official campsite. But I've already gone eighteen and a half, mostly in a light rain, and my feet are begging me to stop. So I do something I very rarely do, hiking down a side trail and then bushwhacking deep into the woods, where I can find a relatively flat piece of ground and "stealth" camp out of sight of the park rangers. Shenandoah National Park set up its network of campsites along the Trail during an earlier, less ambitious backpacking era: they are sited eleven or twelve miles apart, so you either need to do a short day or a twenty-mile plus day, unless you break the rules. Which is fine if you truly leave no trace: no campfire, no breaking or uprooting of branch or brush, some scattering of leaves and duff when you leave so the spot looks as untrammeled as before. Then hope you can find your way back to the Trail.

I enjoy my night away from the beaten path—the rain lets up just long enough for me to set up and cook a quick dinner, then lulls me to sleep with a patter through which I can just hear the little stream nearby. I wake up early hoping to leave in half-light, but something goes very wrong. When I finish boiling water for breakfast and unscrew the propane canister from my backpacking stove, it starts spitting out all of the gas inside with no way to shut it off. Soon I have an empty canister that I was counting on to last until my hike ends back at the Roost in Keys Gap, West Virginia, eight days and 130 miles north. Fortunately there's an upside that, till now, has been a downside.

The deer in the SNP, which starts twenty-five miles back just outside of Waynesboro, appear almost tame at times: no one can hunt them here and, I'm afraid, plenty of park visitors feed them. So they wait on the trail as you approach, as though hoping for a handout, and then bolt at the very last moment. That's the downside: one of the prettiest sections of the Trail is also one of the least wild. The trail parallels and often verges on the heavily touristed Skyline Drive, the hum of traffic never far off. The upside, for chronically hungry thruhikers and now for me, concerns the Waysides that dot the highway, selling "free" calories to the distance hikers (food that doesn't need to be carried, burning nearly as many calories as it supplies), and, I hope, a gas cartridge to me.

Not this time. The only Wayside I'll pass for two days carries every kind of fuel source you can imagine, from RV-sized propone tanks to cans of white gas to 16 ounce cylinders for car camping, but not the little backpacking canister I need. So I stock up on cheese and other stuff I can eat without cooking and hope for better luck at the next Wayside. The walking is easy, gentle ups and downs along a well-marked path, and the day's sixteen miles go by quickly. In addition to the friendly deer I happen on cottontails, chipmunks, and a succession of towhees scratching under the bushes, as well as a few showier birds: just hours into my hike I see both a scarlet tanager and an indigo bunting, one the brightest red and the other the most brilliant blue bird in the American sky. Thrushes sing and rustle in the woods, a red-eyed vireo, a goldfinch, and a black and white warbler all flit by, and once I hear a call like shrill, mad laughter, look up, and spy a pileated woodpecker with its long beak, beady eye, and flaming red crest. Its head in profile, a miniaturized parasaurolophus, looks like exhibit A for the theory that dinosaurs evolved into birds.

I arrive at Hightop shelter in good time, by 3:30, despite the late start and the detour in search of fuel. Inside the shelter, on a shelf high above the Trail register, I see two canisters exactly like the one that failed me that morning, down to the brand (MSR). A quick couple of shakes confirms that one is full, the other half full. I have never seen a usable gas canister in any other shelter on the AT and I never will again. Only this one time, the only time I ever need one.

Distance hikers call this "Trail magic," a term often abused to mean leaving coolers full of jello snack cups and juice boxes at a trail crossing or in a shelter close to the road. Real Trail magic happens, as it does today, when you find the thing you desperately need inexplicably, improbably waiting for you, or handed to you by another hiker, or given without asking by a stranger as you walk through a town. Many AT hikers I meet in the woods have stories just like mine and I will have several more Trail magic experiences of my own over the years to come. Spend enough time on the AT and you come to appreciate the profound interrelatedness of everything that exists and everything that happens, what Buddhists calls pratityasamutpada, the mutual co-arising of the universe in all its complexity. Everything shapes and sustains, as it is shaped and sustained by, everything else, including our minds and our intentions. When you look at the universe this way, strange coincidences come to seem inevitable, and ultimately no more mysterious or magical than having air to breathe, light to see by, firm ground to walk on, gravity to hold us to this miracle of rare device, the Earth.

The sun has come out so I lay out all my wet gear and clothes to dry in the late afternoon warmth, reading and lazing till dinner and then sleeping soundly despite a snoring shelter companion and his growling dog. The next day I hike a very fast twenty miles, eager to meet my brother at Big Meadow Lodge, where I've reserved us a room and where Brian arrives late but with a resupply of food and a vial of Macallan single malt whiskey. A lot of my most memorable trips in the Cascades and Olympics I hiked with Brian, including a few that seem more than a little crazy thirty years later, not least the one that almost got me killed. Whatever came up—a rockslide, a melting ice bridge, a tricky scramble over crumbling rock—we would egg each other on and together we felt invincible, every near miss only adding to our teenage sense of immortality. We learned to trust to the mountains and to one another, though as the older brother Brian usually took the lead.

Now he has taken the lead in aging, apparently saddled (through some perversity of the genes) with my share of ills and injuries on top of his own. His knees, his back, his feet, a ruptured hernia and a scary inflammation in the nerves all take their turn in keeping him from returning to the trail with me. I had fantasized early on that, at least in the mid-Atlantic states near his home base in Maryland, Brian would backpack long stretches with me, but for now even the two mile backpack he did with Shonu two years ago, to meet me in Deer Lick shelter, would be a stretch. So instead he does his part with logistical support, getting me from Ash and Kim's in Carlisle to Waynesboro, then meeting me halfway through my ten day trek, the longest I've done to date, with resupply and stories to share. He drives over 700 miles in a six-day period to help me out—he agrees as soon as I ask him. I wonder if the bond that connects us, one of the very few in my life that I'm certain will last until death, would be as strong if it weren't for our early hiking and mountaineering together. What I do know is that hiking the Olympics and Cascades brought us closer, and something of this mountain brotherhood revives every time we meet up in the Appalachians.

Now carrying six days of food I leave the Lodge early, Brian still fast asleep, to walk another nineteen miles through the Park. The rain early on along with the long days have left one heel and both little toes raw again, but on this friendly terrain they don't bother me much. A redtail hawk flies low overhead, hunting, and I come within a few feet of another small, semi-tame deer. Ash, an amateur naturalist since his teens, has told me that the mid-Atlantic deer have grown, on average, considerably smaller over the past century, the largest bucks favored by hunters, and so cut early out of the gene pool. Aside from humans, though, the deer now have few large predators to worry about, so their numbers grow largely unchecked and the competition for scarce food both shrinks the deer further and in places ravages the forest understory. Nothing a good sprinkling of cougars couldn't take care of, if only they could return.

The next two days were planned as shorter ones, to protect my feet, a reasonable thirteen miles followed by an easy ten-and-a-half. But I finish the first thirteen miles before noon and can't bring myself to stop walking. Along with a group of hikers from the shelter the night before, I decide to go for the twenty-three and a half mile day, though we spread out to walk solo. Alone, I soak in the sights and sounds of the trail, a veery singing from the woods, wild pink azaleas growing along the path, a chance find of no fewer than seven pink lady slippers all clustered together. I just miss meeting several black bears—everyone but me has a bear story when we converge at Tom Floyd shelter at around five in the afternoon. And we all have sore feet, even the trail-hardened young thruhikers.

Backpacking nearly two-dozen miles in a day turns out to be harder psychologically than physically: I'm not sure I can do it, simply because it's more than I've ever done before. I experience a bewildering succession of moods over the ten hours of hiking, often happy or even elated, sometimes discouraged, at times, my blisters acting up, welling with self-pity. I try to watch the passing moods the way I watch the clouds pass, following some advice I've read the night before: "Different winds come from all directions . . . In the same way sensations arise in the body—pleasant or unpleasant or neutral. When the meditator sees sensations as he does the winds . . . he will fully understand them and be free from dependence on them."

As I've collected various items of ultra-light gear for my section hikes—a titanium cooking pot, a two-inch "classic" Swiss Army knife, a two-ounce packcover—I've also collected a small library of what I think of as ultra-light wisdom books. These are little books the size of a deck of cards, Shambhala Pocket Classics, compact and designed for slow, contemplative reading. On this trip I carry the *Pocket Buddha Reader*, a title that for some reason tickles me. Reading and re-reading short sections each night in my tent or in a shelter, I hark back to them on and off as I walk. Some phrases stay with me for days, mantra-like: *Different winds come from all directions; Develop a meditation that is like water;* and one that will run through all my hikes to come. *For there is a path to follow and there is walking to be done, but there is no walker.* These are not exactly phrases to think with. It's more that, as the poet Keats (another of the Romantics I teach) puts it, they tease us out of thought.

The long day takes me nearly out of the Park and into more varied terrain, farmland and meadows followed by a more rugged, rockier section and then soft hiking on a path nearly hidden under forest duff. At the end of an eighteen mile day I find myself alone again at Dick's Dome shelter, enjoying the late afternoon music: woodpeckers drilling, a hermit thrush singing, the shelter stream rippling, deer ticks dropping from the trees. I brush these off but not, it seems, all of them. At the end of the next day's more reasonable fifteen miles, I balance on a rock mid-stream to soak my feet in the cold rush of water and spot a deer tick firmly attached to my inner thigh, hidden by my hiking shorts till now. The little Swiss Army classic, small as it is, includes a pair of tweezers that I use to wrench the tick out—leaving the head behind. (I should have rubbed it with Vaseline first, to loosen its hold, but I didn't want to budge from the cool stream.) Now there's nothing for it but to dig the head out with the point of the tiny blade, a mouse's sword, bloody but effective. The tick inspires a quick census of my various bites—I've been stung or gnawed on by mosquitos, gnats, spiders, and horse flies, but none of them itch half as much as the bite of a New England black fly so I take it all in stride.

The bugs have flourished as the temperatures have heated up over the last two days, and I in contrast begin to wilt. The hike's final seventeen miles, partly over the Devil's Roller Coaster (a series of ups and downs that reminds me Vermont), has me dragging, though I speed up after I've called Ash from the top of one of the many hills. I'm arriving a day early, and it turns out he and Kim won't be there yet, so I begin pushing to get to the little store at Keys Gap, a mile past Ash's cabin, before it closes for the evening. I arrive just in time to grab a gallon of water (the Roost has no plumbing), a six pack of Yuengling, and pint of ice cream, all of which I drag, along with my pack, back up to the ridge. After the ice cream and a beer or two, I knock on the door of Ash's nearest neighbor, a quarter mile up the dirt road, who invites me in for a much needed shower. Back at the Roost, locked out of the cabin, I look for a decent patch of ground to pitch my tent—all the terrain around proves either too rocky or too slanted or both.

Then I notice the Cocktail Platform, a freestanding wooden deck Ash and Kim have built into the hillside overlooking the Shenandoah River. My ultralight tent, not much bigger than a good-sized coffin, just fits. I angle it so that the mesh gives me a view of the river snaking through the late afternoon haze below, an uncertain green shading into purple as the shadows seep into the valley. I leave the tent-fly off so that the breezes can flow through and then I wait for the stars to come out.

March 2008. The snow flurries start almost as soon as Dawn turns back after walking the first half mile with me. It's the last week of March, a few days after the vernal equinox, but winter has not yet given in, even here in Davenport Gap, just north of the Great Smoky Mountains. The maple trees have yet to leaf in, though Dawn spotted an early violet at the trailhead. Again I will walk the North Carolina-Tennessee line, heading north 123 miles to Iron Mountain Gap. The streams are running well but still easy to cross, snowflakes float through the bare woods, and the cold stays in the pleasant range until the top of Snowbird Mountain, at over 4000 feet, when the winds whip up and the snowfall thickens. I skip lunch, pull on my rain parka and hiking gloves, and move quickly down the mountain toward shelter as a good inch of snow builds up underfoot, something I never anticipated, but easy enough to manage with a hiking stick I pull from the woods. At 3:30 a small crowd of thruhikers has already gathered at Groundhog Creek Shelter in Deep Gap. That's when I pick up my new, and first legitimate, trail name.

According to best AT custom, a trail name should not be chosen but bestowed, spontaneously, by another distance hiker. (A custom often ignored.) So after passing for several years as Cascader, I decide before this hike to drop my self-chosen alias and just see what happens. It does not take long. One of the thruhikers, a middle-aged woman, asks me my trail name and I tell her, "I don't have one, but you can call me Al." She turns and shouts out to the others, busy building a fire, "Hey, everybody, this is Call Me Al." Perfect. For the rest of my AT hiking days, when anyone asks my name, I'll be able to say "I'm Call Me Al. Or, you can just call me Al."

I get plenty of chances to practice as one after another hiker arrives out of the snow until the shelter fills and a handful of tents pop up around it. Most are thruhikers who started at Springer Mountain, 250 miles back, in late February—hiking many days in the snow. Statistically, up to half of these will never finish the Trail and I'm struck by the greenness of some, who may never have backpacked or spent a night in the woods before a few weeks ago. As questions come up, about gear, about the Trail up ahead, about basic woodcraft, and I keep answering them, one of them, a tall, bearded forty year old with a booming voice, asks me just how I know all this. And I realize I've already hiked over seven hundred miles of the AT, making me the old hand among a crowd of rookies. Though I'm careful not to point this out—in fact, I hold my tongue for the rest of the evening. At night, as the temperature falls to 20 degrees, a barred owl and a great horned owl take turns hooting from the woods. Later, I wake up to a hellish racket as a nightjar calls out *chuck-will's-widow*, swoops to the ground, and then fights for its life against some mistaken prey turned predator, a fox or a weasel. Uncanny screams fill the air for a few long minutes, then utter silence.

After another inch of snow overnight the woods glisten, fresh white powder on the ground, on the bare trees, on the glossy green leaves of the rhododendrons that start to appear now. No spring blooms as yet, no thrushes or ovenbirds calling, no stinging bugs either, but lots to enjoy, the clearing skies, the evergreen shrubs and trees (for now, just scattered hemlocks), delicate needle ice pushing up from the ground, the morning sun picking out innumerable glints in the snow. The trail climbs up Max Patch, a classic bald, with open views in every direction, then heads down steeply—I grab a new stick to keep from slipping on the snow and mud underfoot. At night, camping on top of Walnut Mountain, the stars come out brightly, mirrored below by the lights of a city glowing in the distance, probably Hot Springs, thirteen miles northeast. The night grows warmer instead of colder and by morning the snow has vanished.

The warming trend continues as the trail descends and then climbs, a thousand feet, up Bluff Mountain, then a long descent, broken by a few ups, way down to Hot Springs, almost 3000 feet below my overnight perch. I've rented a "primitive" style cottage on the edge of Spring Creek for Dawn and me. I turn on my phone long enough to call my kids and make sure they're OK, and then call Lori in Seattle to check on Dad. Dawn arrives with my resupply in tow as I sit on the porch under the trees and we walk to the Paddler's Pub for an early dinner. Then we soak, naked, in one of the hot tubs at the mineral springs, before retiring early for a rustic evening in the cabin, the windows open to let in the breeze and the stream sounds. In the morning, after a quick breakfast, Dawn heads back to Asheville and her kitchen job while I start the long climb out of Hot Springs, about 3500 feet, as the day quickly heats up to nearly 70 degrees. Over four days of walking, the lingering winter has completely given way to summery heat.

The trail rises through long stretches of rhododendrons mixed in with stands of small, stressed-looking pines surrounded by mounds of brown needles. I pass several dry water sources and fill up at a pooled spring, not on the map, about three miles before my campsite. The trail levels for a while to pass an old tobacco field, now a nature preserve, where a bluebird flits near the house someone's built for him. Higher up, I step over bear scat and, soon after, the trace of a fox or bobcat.

Climbing in the heat quickly becomes a trudge and I find my third hiking stick of the trip just off the trail some 500 feet above Hot Springs. I like this one, a strong, slightly misshapen hardwood branch, ash or oak, knotted and just the right size and weight. I trim it some with my climbing knife and quickly become attached to it as it helps me, physically or psychologically or both, manage the steep ups and the trickier downs. By the end of the week it's like a fifth limb. It will go with me on the Trail for a thousand miles to come.

The next day the trail gets rougher and much less crowded. The whole group of thruhikers I started out with must have hunkered down in Hot Springs for an extra day or two of rest and calorie dosing. The one distance hiker I've met since then, the General, a brawny and genial ex-British commando, has probably left me ten miles behind by now. I'll have campsites all to myself for three of the next four nights. And many miles of solitary walking.

Hiking alone, up mountains, over rocky ridgelines, down into gaps, across creeks, and up again, I let myself relax into states of mind often called meditative (though I find the term "meditation" less helpful the more I engage in the activity itself). I have an unexpected guide this trip in Gary Snyder's *Practice of the Wild*, a book I've brought along for its edgy, provocative takes on concepts like nature, wilderness, and even walking itself—"That's the way to see the world: in our own bodies." But I did not expect to learn so much from Snyder's nature book about Zen Buddhism. Especially about Dōgen, one of the greatest of all the Zen ancestors and one with special affinities for Snyder, who at times all but channels him. Although Snyder's essay on Dōgen's *Mountains and Rivers Sutra* speaks most directly to this trip—challenging me to see the mountains walking—I find myself returning still more to a phrase from the *Genjō Kōan*, dropped almost casually into the end of an earlier chapter. "To carry yourself forward and experience myriad things is delusion. That myriad things come forth and experience themselves is awakening." What does it mean to walk fifteen or twenty miles a day without carrying yourself forward? What does it mean to stop experiencing nature so you can better appreciate the way the things of nature experience themselves?

A grouse drums from the underbrush close to my feet. Last night's big downpour has ended but mist rises from the damp forest on both sides of the ridge—the distant lines of mountains shade to blue in the haze. The rhododendron buds have grown bigger, swollen with petals still held tightly within. High up in the trees a sharp tapping punctuates the silence as a hidden woodpecker drills for grubs. Moss gleams greenly between coarse-grained rocks, water from a spring trickles underneath. A small knot near the top of my stick rubs the beginnings of a blister just above my fourth knuckle—shifting the stick restores the feeling of smooth wood. At the shelter, at the end of a long fifteen miles, a junco scratches the earth in front of the overhang and a small cottontail creeps out from the brush to sit placidly a few feet away. Slowly the light drains from the sky as shadows mass together in the woods. Near midnight another rainstorm moves through the mountains, coyotes howling in between the squalls.

The rains continue much of the next day, giving way to periods of mist, and the springs and streams perk up. Down to just a few days of food, my backpack feels weightless again except during the steeper climbs. Despite the scattered rain, my boots and socks stay dry and my feet blissfully unblistered. Coming to another empty shelter, I rip away the tattered tarp some previous hikers have used to keep out the cold and late snow. I like the front open to the woods.

The temperature drops again, close to freezing, and the next morning brings another surprise. Walking across Big Bald the mist blows in so thickly that it turns me around and I have to backtrack until I can find the way north again.

Once found, the trail descends through bare woods covered with rime ice—a fairy forest. Then a series of gentler ascents and descents on broad, level, park-like stretches of trail. By late afternoon I've covered twenty miles. Sometimes I manage to lose myself in the walking. Hiking up, I let the mountain flow down past me; the ridgelines stream by and the lines of distant mountains gather like waves. "If you doubt mountains walking," Dōgen says, "you do not know your own walking."

I find it tempting, walking with his words floating through my head, to identify with Snyder, fast becoming another of my heroes. Snyder spent much of his childhood in North Seattle, living a mile or two from the house I grew up in; like me, he learned to love the mountains by hiking and backpacking in the North Cascades and the Olympics. And like mine, his interest in Zen Buddhism began at an early age, in my case at seventeen, in Snyder's as an undergraduate at Reed. That interest took both of us to the Bay Area as young men, Snyder to the Asian Studies program at Berkeley, me to the San Francisco Zen Center. But there the similarities end. While Snyder went on to spend several years in Japanese monasteries and then devote his adulthood to poetry, activism, nature writing, and his own eclectic, deeply serious form of Zen practice, I spent a little less than a year at the Zen Center before leaving in despair. It took me three decades to find my way back to formal Zen practice, half a lifetime.

Yet here I was, walking with Snyder, walking with Dōgen, walking with the mountains walking.

The next day, an easy ten and a half miles, I stop at the bottom of a deep gap at Uncle Johnny's hostel on the Nolichucky River—Uncle Johnny himself rents me a towel and leads me to the shower stalls. He also sells me three Snickers Bars for the archaic price of 40 cents each—after eight days in the woods, I've gotten a taste of the distance hiker's remorseless hunger. Then back into the woods through hemlocks and pines, mountain laurel and rhododendron, and the occasional bare hardwood. I take it easy and look for a stream to soak my T-shirt in. I sleep alone in the ungainly No Business Knob shelter, preferring not to camp because of all the dead trees around, widow makers poised to fall on any unsuspecting tent. At night the wind comes up and one huge snag just a few feet away groans ominously with every blast.

I hike in total solitude the next day, seeing no one at all until I reach Iron Mountain Gap, where Jim McGavran showed me a red trillium two years earlier. I arrive at 4:25, five minutes before I asked Dawn to meet me, and she pulls up fifteen minutes later. Dawn asks me about the hike, looking at me quizzically, and I tell her, guessing she will understand, "some Zen stuff was happening on the trail." She just smiles back, adding "I could see it in your eyes," and then we drop the subject and get into her car to drive back to Asheville. The weather has heated up again and we enjoy the warm North Carolina evening together, splitting a pizza and drinking the local ale, celebrating the first day of April.

May 2009. Sunfish Pond looks so clear and placid and blue that I want to take off my pack and jump in despite the cool weather. It's a round tarn carved out by the last ice age, the southernmost of a whole chain of glacial pools, ponds, and lakes that lie alongside the Trail from here north to Daicey Pond at the foot of Katahdin. It's like finding a vintage piece of northern New England dropped into western New Jersey. But the sky clouds up again, the temperature drops back to the low 50s, and I've gotten a late start, so I keep going after a long, dreamy break by the shore.

Two hours and six miles earlier Jessica, my nephew Leon's wife, dropped me off at the Delaware Water Gap. I'm feeling happy to find myself alone in the woods again, at the start of a 150 mile trek that will take me through the New Jersey section of the Trail and almost all of the New York section, a bit of which I backpacked the week before to make for an endpoint closer to Leon and Jessica's home in Connecticut, where Leon teaches and coaches hockey at the Taft School. And where the male students, I discovered, all seem to idolize him. They call him "Coach"—if he ever wants to join me on a hike, he's already got his trail name.

Once north of the Delaware Water Gap the Trail corridor through both states can grow quite narrow, sometimes taking to paved roads, sometimes threading its way through local parks, sometimes skirting suburban back yards. For that very reason, though, the chances get higher for animal sightings—the critters here don't have much habitat left—and many hikers encounter their first rattlesnake here and maybe, like Mountain Dog, their first bear. Sadly, I meet no rattlesnake on this hike, though I do see garter snakes and, at one point, two large black snakes slithering across the path just ahead of me. No bear, either, but any number of small, wary deer and nervous cottontails, as well as an Eastern mole, a moving bundle of soft grey fur, that runs quickly on its short legs just ahead of my boots.

I sleep that first night in a Mohican Center bunkroom, hearing a whippoorwill calling in the dark, and start the first of several twenty-mile days to come. I'm struck this day, as I hike in solitude, by the impossibility of my goal—hiking the whole Appalachian Trail, passing every white blaze. In fact, there is no complete and entire Trail—its very length changes each year through re-routings planned and unplanned (one day in Connecticut I have to roadwalk around a derailed train sprawled over the green corridor). The white blazes themselves fade out or the trees they're painted on fall down, and somewhere some Trail maintainer may be adding new ones as I walk. And I think of some of the ways I've seen the footpath transformed, into a running stream climbing Greylock, into a river of leaves with no discernable edges walking through the Vermont woods, into an obstacle path of blowdowns and overhangs hiking up Cube Mountain in spring, or buried under three feet of snow near Crawford Notch. The Trail flows and eddies, changing as I change, changing just from the fact of my walking it, changing me as I walk. There is no trail. There is no walker.

A big cottontail scampers by, one of many signs that spring has arrived: towhees and ovenbirds calling in the woods, wild orchids just off the path, wild pink azaleas in bloom, one mountain laurel sporting small white flowers that must have opened just this morning. I hike in T-shirt and shorts, wanting my arms and legs bare despite the residual chill in the air; at night, the temperature drops almost to freezing. But the spring will not be denied and the trees around the shelter I sleep in are all freshly and fully leaved, a brilliant and intense green that will fade and mellow in the summer heat to come.

The next day the temperature climbs into the 70s and the first thrushes begin singing, invisible, from the bushes and trees that line the footpath. I come to High Point shelter early—this is the rare short day, thirteen miles, on this long hike—where you can spy New York City in the distance, though today the city is lost in a low haze. Still, the sun shines directly overhead and I walk downstream to give myself a good washing, then fill a large, packable canteen with water and unroll a collapsible bowl to do some laundry in the woods away from the water source. Sitting at the shelter's picnic table after dinner, I spot a flash of pink through the trees: five pink lady slippers growing near the stream, with three more in a row higher up on the bank and a solitary one a bit further off. I fall asleep listening to stream sounds, thrush songs, and the occasional airplane passing far overhead.

And then the temperature climbs still higher, into the 80s, before I've gotten well into what I've planned as a twenty-four mile day. I hadn't expected such warm weather in May, and now I feel my full age in the heat. The long day's hike is varied, moving through forest, pasture land, marshes dotted with bog bridges, a wildlife refuge, road walks, and a long, winding boardwalk over a final marsh before returning to woodlands and climbing 800 feet up Wawayanda Mountain. Said "mountain" is really more of a big hill, but after battling the heat, finding scant water sources, fending off a dozen different species of biting insects in the swampy refuge, and walking over twenty miles, the modest climb uses up my last bit of energy. For the first time I stop short of my intended mark for the day, camping on top of the mountain, hidden off trail in the scrubby woods, rather than hike another three miles to the shelter. The stealth campsite makes for a quiet, solitary evening, but the feeling of total exhaustion makes me question the way I've planned this hike.

And for good reason. Months earlier, sitting with maps and guidebooks at home, I'd noted the low elevations for this section—no point rising even to 2000 feet, much of the terrain under 1000—and decided that, to make the hike interesting, I'd cover not my usual fourteen to fifteen miles but something between seventeen and eighteen per day. And not only that: I would carry all nine days of food with me, avoiding town stops entirely and starting out with what turned out to be thirty-eight pounds on my back. This would not have been considered a heavy pack in my youth—though we were already experimenting with the lighter weight gear starting to crop up at the REI Co-op on Capitol Hill in Seattle, then the only REI store there was. But anything under a third of your own weight was long considered fine, and even on day one my backpack weighs in at just under a fourth of mine. Though my feet stay blister free in the dry conditions, the combination of extra weight on my back and longer miles leaves me more not less tired each day, especially once the heat kicks in. And the days to come stay hot. So hot that the water sources quickly start to give out.

After cutting day four short on Wawayanda I find it harder to forget about my backpack, which I typically don't notice at all on anything like level ground. It grows harder to lose myself in the walking, harder to give myself to the trail. But the hike never becomes an endless slog, let alone a death march, though the dry conditions make that a literal possibility. Crossing the state line into New York the trail climbs onto a rocky ridgeline under a hot sun. The few running streams are down to trickles and, at these low elevations, I treat what water I find with pills that give it the chlorinated taste of an accidental gulp from the town swimming pool. Even then I find the water a little dubious and for once find myself worrying about contamination, though at Wildcat Shelter, where I spend the night, the shelter spring flows nicely, straight from the rock, and I drink it untreated, as I do nearly all spring water. Today, I'm happy to find water here at all, as more than one southbounder tells me that a number of the shelters further north have gone dry.

That night the shelter lives up to its name as a bobcat screams from a few yards away, stopping on its way to the spring, I guess, as it prowls south toward Cat Rocks.

The next day it takes twelve hours to cover nineteen and a half miles, an embarrassingly slow pace, not least when a tough old distance hiker breezes past me—I don't get his name, but I learn somehow that he's about to turn 70. Nothing for it but to keep putting one foot ahead of the other and just let my pace be what it is. I see my first oriole of the season, perched high among bright green maple leaves, its song breezy and chaotic like a robin's, but in the pure soprano tones of a robin that's gone to opera school. Chipmunks skitter about everywhere, energetic as always despite the heat. Most water sources have run dry and the few streams still running are too low to fill a water bottle to the brim. Every chance encounter now includes some talk about water, where to find it, where it's stopped flowing, how little there is in general. All of us hikers have bonded together in a community of thirst.

I sleep at a dry shelter that's been trashed by weekend partiers, too close to the road. In front of the shelter someone has left an open gallon jug, a third filled with brackish water, probably from the pooled spring before it gave out. (For now it's been reduced to a mudhole covered over with leaves.) Half crazy with thirst, I can't stop myself from taking a few long swigs before I treat the rest, adding it to the liter I've been hoarding to cook with. For the first time in my life, I truly understand the preciousness of water; for a long time to come I'll stop letting the faucet run while I brush my teeth. The deer must be regularly fed here because they walk right into the campsite looking for a handout. I wake up in the middle of the night in time to scare off a large roof rat nosing its way toward my sleeping bag.

The next day the trail makes a slight climb up Bear Mountain, a local attraction. The promised water fountain has been shut off but two friendly women, out for a stroll, give me all the water from one of their canteens. Not long after the trail merges with a walkway along Hessian Lake, apparently a very popular picnic site, because everywhere I pass families, of virtually every American ethnicity, sharing outdoor tables teeming with food. Though I'm happy to see such unexpected bounty two years into the Great Recession, I'm a little put off that no one offers me so much as a soda or potato chip, famished and parched as I must look after a week on the Trail. I pass among them like a hungry ghost. Then the trail, bizarrely, heads directly through a zoo, skirting caged animals from the Northeastern woods, possums and beavers and black bears. I get as many stares as the creatures. Probably my smell by now is just as strong.

Finally the trail crosses the Hudson River on the Bear Mountain highway bridge, noisy with cars and trucks but still splendid with the great river spread out below, broad and magnificent. I reach Greymoor Abbey, a bit off the trail, by four, where the monks have set aside a pavilion and part of a ball field for AT hikers. I fill my bottles from a spigot and take a deliciously cold shower as the sky clouds up. A former distance hiker shows up in a van with cases of cold beer and hot dogs to grill. So us hikers get to have some picnic food after all. I tent out at the far edge of the field with a light, half-hearted rain spattering the tentfly, wishing it would get heavier, wishing water to come pouring, streaming out of the dark sky.

The cloudburst finally arrives the next day. Down to only two days of food and perked up by the monks' hospitality the evening before, I return to something like my usual pace, covering nineteen miles in ten hours. I see the usual deer and rabbits and still more wild orchids, as well as leopard frogs and squat American toads, out searching for water perhaps, as I walk through hardwoods on rocky paths and old woods roads. The thunder begins booming when I'm about an hour from the RPH shelter so I speed up, making real time, trying to beat the rain. With less than a mile to go the storm hits hard, drenching me and everything around me with rain, big sheets of rain, and all I feel is elation: cool at last! The shelter, sited just across from someone's back yard, looks like a former carriage house, with a door and a pump outside. The pump water has a metallic, rusty taste and I drink up lustily. The shelter is filled to overflowing, with weekenders (it's a Sunday), distance hikers, and a group of Bentley College girls out for five days on the Trail. Cornbread, a thruhiker I met at the Abbey, breaks out his banjo and serenades them with a rousing, off-key version of "Amy." Meanwhile a father and son team try in vain to get control of their black lab, mechanically chasing an endless supply of frisky cottontails out front. Cornbread and I end up sleeping on the floor. It's a crazy last night on the trail.

The next day I find Leon and Jess waiting for me under the Dover Oak, perhaps the largest tree on the entire AT, 114 feet tall and wide as a freight car, a lonely relic of the ancient Northeastern forest. They ask me if there's anything I've been craving and I answer, "ice cream," so they take me to a local place with a dozen homemade flavors and I end up choosing a huge strawberry milkshake with a banana on the side. But first I ask for an extra large cup of water.

May 2011. As I leave Ash behind, climbing up to the ridge under a dwindling rain, it already feels strange to be heading south instead of north. All my longer hikes have moved in the classic direction, away from Springer and toward Katahdin, but for once I head southbound, crossing paths with the leaders of this year's northbound pack and months ahead of any southbound early birds who managed to leave Katahdin before June. Ash and I only reached the Delaware Water Gap after 11, which is fine, because I only plan to hike 6.8 miles today. Then nine more days and another 164 miles will take me back to the Boiling Springs Tavern, waiting for Ash to take me to Creekside, where he and Kim have found the antique country home of their dreams across the road from a dairy farm.

Everyone talks about the rocks in northern Pennsylvania but the trail rising out of the Gap is a woodland path, the trees around just leafed in, the rocky stretches still to the south. In fact, after the White Mountains and southern Maine, the rocks will strike me as rather tame—if southbounders dominated Trail culture the way northbounders do, I doubt anyone would have had much to say about the infamous rocks of PA. Or maybe, in my case, it's also having grown up hiking the North Cascades, where scrambling up an old rock slide or inching across a fresh one makes part of any ordinary day. Birdsong fills the sky with the warbler wave coming through—I spot dozens of drab colored warblers I can't identify apart from the ovenbirds, out in force. A smallish wood turtle ambles across the trail, its shell a rough mosaic of clamshell-sized pieces, while chipmunks dart into the brush and squirrels make scolding noises from the trees. Wild pink azaleas are in full bloom and purplish-pink spring beauties, with their five delicately veined petals, dot the woods all around. Just a few yards from my intended campsite a scarlet tanager flashes brightly in the late afternoon sun, then disappears into the trees.

I spend the night in a large shelter that fills up with a whole assortment of hikers, including a small group of scouts with their dads and one sixteen-year-old sister who won't be left behind. She stays close to her father, calling him "Daddy" in a way that pierces my heart each time. It's partly with envy, as the days of my own daughter backpacking with me have decidedly ended for now. And it's partly with grief, as it's been slightly less than a month since I spent a very long morning at my father's bedside, with my hand lightly resting on his shoulder, listening for his last breath, watching the life slowly ebb out of him.

Over the next few days the rocks come and go but never strike me as all that formidable. Hiking down into and then back up out of a succession of deep, deep gaps—these I find more challenging than the rocks—I see fewer wildflowers than expected but more birds. Sitting in front of a shelter with a trail toughened section hiker, Jake, I point out a scarlet tanager and he tells me about the first one he ever saw, further south on the Trail, so bright red he assumed it was some tropical exotic blown far out of range by a storm. The next day an indigo bunting flits through the woods, later a Cooper's hawk flies directly at me down the trail before swooping up over my head, and still later, at Outerbridge shelter, a very loud whippoorwill wakes up the whole campsite at first light. Unable to get back to sleep, I leave the shelter early in a light rain to walk another seventeen miles south.

The weekend is past, the scouts and other weekenders gone home, and I walk for miles without encountering another human being. Along with lots of wild azaleas in bloom I begin to see more evergreen shrubs, rhododendrons and mountain laurels with newly opened, still tiny flowers. Here white pines crowd out the deciduous trees and, heightened by the rain and mist, the woods take on a deeper, more durable shade of green. Now the rocks get more interesting, sharp and rainslicked, and I rely more on my stick, that and a well-known voice in my head. When I take a long moment to begin the tricky passage over the Knife Edge, a sharp, narrow granite ridge with a dropoff on either side, the voice says, "Just keep going, Al, this is nothing you haven't done plenty of times before." When one boot slips as I side step down Bake Oven Knob, the same voice talks me down: "Now, Al, if you're going to fall, wait and fall when you get to the bottom, so you won't break anything." This time the words actually come out of my mouth, which is strange, because the voice isn't mine. It's Dad's.

Hike alone long enough and you are certain to hear voices. Some of these are simple illusions, tricks the woods start to play on you when you haven't heard another human voice for a day or two. You hear light laughter ahead of you on the trail, a girl's or young woman's, and then you come to a fast stream making high pitched music as it runs through a stony channel. Or the rumbling tones of a man's deep voice come to you from around a bend, until you make the turn in the trail and see a large bumblebee lazily gathering pollen from a knot of wildflowers. It can be the throaty call of a raven, or the noise of one branch rubbing against another in a steady wind, or the shriek of the wind itself.

And sometimes the voices come from inside instead of outside, from memory and longing, though they can seem just as unwilled as the stream sounds and windblasts. For me it's always someone I hiked with for years in my youth in Washington State. Sometimes my best friend Scott, sometimes my brother Brian. But most often it's Dad's voice, which is odd, because I spent a lot more time in the woods with both Scott and Brian than I did with my father. But maybe not odd at all, since it was Dad who led me to the mountains, who took me on my first overnights, and who was with me when I still needed lots of guidance and help and plain encouragement. And it's mainly when I hit a rough patch that his voice speaks to me now.

After four days on the trail the sights and sounds begin to come to me without my needing to look or listen for them. The now familiar array of spring birds, the chance encounter on the trail (the nervy deer, the turn-on-a-dime cottontails, a woodchuck ambling obliviously ahead, a spotted toad, a red eft), the alternating stretches of pine and hardwood, of rock and glade. I come to a shelter with a young squatter, barely eighteen years old, with a sweet smile and a broken machete, no tent, no raingear, dug in and cadging food—something that's not supposed to happen, but the Great Recession has made the Trail an alternative to urban homelessness. Trail culture generally has gone downhill over the past few years—more cell phone use within earshot of other hikers, more throwing of rinse water on the ground instead of drinking it or tossing it into the woods, more cooking inside the shelters during bear season. And more hikers than ever before—a night alone, once easy to come by in May, has become a rare treat.

Sometimes the trail goes over sharp rocks, sometimes foot hardened earth, sometimes the smooth, flat stones of an old streambed. The temperature rises to the low 80s and, on my seventh day of hiking, I feel hungry and a little slow. I take eight hours to walk the fifteen miles to the 501 Shelter, a little piece of town on the Trail with four walls and a door, a solar shower, and even pizza delivery (the shelter, a converted barn, sits at a highway crossing). It also has a mirror over the sink and I see my own face for the first time in a week. It's my face and it's not my face. As my ultralight wisdom reading for this hike I've been carrying a miniaturized version of a collection I haven't read since my teens, *Zen Flesh, Zen Bones,* which includes a dated translation of the great koan collection, *The Gateless Gate.* As I back away from the mirror my head spins with the questions from two different koans: "What is your original face before your parents were born" and "Why does Bodhidharma have no beard?" One becomes instantly clear. One remains mysterious but the mystery deepens in interesting ways. Later, I turn on my cellphone long enough to order two large cheese pizzas, take two slices, and give the rest to a trio of young, lean thruhikers much hungrier than I could be.

A big storm blows through overnight—later, I meet two northbounders who had to hunker down under a highway bridge as a tornado ripped across the Trail fifty miles further south. Here the effects are more pleasant than destructive—streams running high (I put on my Crocs to wade one), red efts out in force, scented air (flowers, sweet grasses, the pungent, rain drenched earth itself). I get a second wind which comes none too soon as the Trail plunges a thousand feet down to Swatara Gap, then climbs 900 feet back up, only to descend another 700 to Rauch Gap, once the site of a coal mining town and now almost entirely reclaimed by the woods. The trail follows the old railway bed and coal chips speckle the ground. The cozy shelter here has a nesting phoebe, the first I've seen on this hike; she flits in and out under the eaves until dusk.

Sunday, the last full day of this hike, starts out sprinkly, then just overcast, then misty and hazy, until at last, after a big weather altering wind blows itself out, the sun comes out for good some time before noon. The trail continues to ring its own series of changes, from woodland path to rocky defile, climbing and plunging, until it drops a good thousand feet down to the Susquehanna River. I cross with the highway on the long Clarks Ferry Bridge and, before I'm a third of the way across, a peregrine falcon leaves the opposite shore and comes flying toward me. It hovers above me a moment and then folds in its wings to dive directly at me, calling out angrily: *"skreeeee skreeeee skreeeee skreek skreek!"* Defending its nest at the far end of the bridge, it comes at me again and again, a dozen, two dozen, fifty times or more. Sometimes it swoops down from in front of me, sometimes from behind, sometimes from directly overhead, sometimes it tries to surprise me by appearing suddenly from under the bridge. It comes so close I can clearly see its yellow talons, the zebra stripes on its breast, and the dark and light bars across its tail feathers. I'm glad I've brought my trusty oak branch along and, every time the falcon dives at me, I raise it a foot or two over my head like a lightning rod. I can hear the wind in the bird's feathers but it always stays just clear of the stick. Finally I reach the end of the bridge and the falcon flies up into a tall tree on the south bank, waiting for the next two-legged threat to lumber across.

I stop in Duncannon at the Doyle Hotel, a famous, funky Trail hostel, for a shower, a beer, and a burger before climbing the steep ascent, 800 feet in a bit over a mile, to Hawk Rock and the Cove Mountain shelter a mile beyond. The shelter edge and lower parts of the vertical beams have been well chewed so I expect a porcupine, which duly visits at 11 p.m.—Fat Jim, my chance companion of the night sleeping below, wakes me by saying in his husky voice, "Al, that porky's here." "Where?" "Right in the bunk beneath you." Then I hear the rustling and hope it's not climbing my way.

I weigh a smooth, flat stone in one hand, big enough to deter but much too small to maim, and flick on my headlamp with the other hand. But before I can start pelting it the porcupine scurries back out of the shelter toward the trees. Apparently the local porkies are much less brazen then their cousins up in the cold Berkshires. After that, nothing larger than a mosquito troubles the shelter for a time, and even the bugs stop biting around midnight. Two hours later the mice come out from a rift in the wood near my head. It's just one of those nights, the Trail's way of saying goodbye.

The next day, hiking twenty-one and a half miles to Boiling Springs, I make a decision that proves both shortsighted and potentially fatal. I leave the shelter before 7 a.m. and follow the trail through the woods, down a gentle descent, then a series of fields, where I see a doe with its fawn, and uphill again to Darlington Shelter, where I stop for my first break. A late sleeping northbounder tells me that the spring is running, but it's a long hike down to it, close to a thousand steep feet. I take a swallow from one of my two Nalgenes and decide to wait for the next good spring. None ever appears. Which means backpacking over twenty miles on two liters of water.

After a bit more climbing the trail tops out at 1200 feet and heads back down toward the valley, again through a mix of fields and old woods roads in narrow corridors, and then along a muddy, low river that I don't dare get water from, between the agricultural runoff and heavy metals. The heat builds steadily and the trail cuts through fields in the open sun, then crosses no fewer than three highways (I-81, US11, and the Pennsylvania Turnpike) on hot asphalt. Finally the trail angles sharply down to an unplanned water crossing, a channel of brown runoff water that I wade through, up to my knees, in my Crocs. Far from even considering it a source of potable water, I worry instead that it will infect some of the many cuts and bug bites covering my legs after ten days on the trail.

I lace my boots up and walk on, once more through fields and narrow stands of trees. At one point an old man, walking his little granddaughter by the hand, passes me on a narrow path through an alfalfa field; in his other hand he carries a large cooler, at least two gallons. I look at it longingly and he asks me how I am: I say, "thirsty." He chuckles and moves on. It occurs to me that, under extreme enough conditions, a man might well kill for a few pints of water. Earlier, where a bend in the trail skirts the edge of a town, I had passed an open gate in a fence behind which an afternoon picnic was going in full swing. I wanted to ask for water but worried that the Trail neighbors might see this as an intrusion, come to resent the Trail even more than they no doubt already did, so I move on. I have no way of knowing that, apart from the old man, this is my very last chance for water before Boiling Springs. I also don't know, until Ash tells me later, that by mid-afternoon I'm walking in 95 degree heat; had I known, I would have lost any shyness and asked for water as my human right.

Instead I sip at my last liter bottle, down to two cups, then one and a half, then one, then half a cup, and I let my breath and body take over as ordinary consciousness drops away and my mind enters what I call the dreamtime. It's not a symptom of dehydration—at least I don't think it is—but a kind of defense, as though conscious thought has gotten just too expensive to keep up under the circumstances. I cross paths with two more groundhogs, listen to towhees and cardinals, pass forgotten stone houses grown over with vines. I walk on steadily, beyond worry, determined that I'll survive this day and needing only to keep going. Finally I reach the outskirts of Boiling Springs and call Ash, who tells me that the Boiling Springs Tavern, sadly, has closed for the week. But the Appalachian Trail Conservancy has a regional office there with an outdoor faucet for the use of passing hikers. I wait for Ash on a shaded bench, drinking lukewarm, tinny water by the liter. Before long Ash and I are back at Creekside, just the two of us, drinking Lord Chesterfield ales and plunging back into our conversation about books and writing, nature and the Trail, various birds and animals we've seen, our lives, and whatever comes up next, the conversation we've been keeping up for twenty-five years.

May 2012. I pull into Standing Bear by mid-afternoon, having spent the night before at Creekside with Ash and Kim. I drop my sleeping bag and a duffel with my hiking clothes in the bunkhouse and park my car above the hostel on a patch of grass well above stream level, just in case it floods. A lot can happen in two and a half weeks. In the bunkhouse I let my copy of *A Zen Wave*, Robert Aitken's dharma talks on various haiku by Bashō, fall open at random just to see what pops up. This poem:

Let my name
Be traveler;
First rains.

Let my name be "Call Me Al"; the Trail beckons. Inspired by Bashō I decide to compose haiku on the trail, at least one or two each day, and transcribe them at night into my trail journal.

That evening I make a bargain with Curtis, the pony-tailed, Trail-savvy owner, for a ride all the way to Springer Mountain in Georgia the next day, 180 miles: he charges me half of what I tell him I'm ready to pay. His stepson Ian drives me early the next morning and I'm on the Approach Trail well before noon, a nine mile, two thousand foot climb up from the Amicalola Falls State Park visitor center. The approach trail is optional but traditional (you can catch the trail higher up and one thruhiker actually had himself airdropped onto the top of Springer), so I dutifully mount the steps alongside the Falls and eventually find myself on the summit, where the AT officially begins. Then a quicker three miles to Stover Creek shelter, through woods filled with ovenbirds and other warblers, wild azaleas—both pink and flame—in bloom, the mountain laurels just coming into flower. This has become my favorite wildflower: a delicate cup made of five petals, joined just below the pointed tops, white with a slight pink tinge, with ten stamens running up slight channels in the middle of each petal and at each joint between, a fine red line running around the bottom of the cup swelling into ten tiny points where the stamens push up. From further away, the flowers are fairy cups; from close up, ten-pointed stars. I'm here just at the right time.

Except for those spring rains Bashō mentioned, which start in the afternoon, grow harder overnight, and won't let up all day. I've planned only twelve miles for my first full day to give my feet a chance to harden up, but my boots and socks are soaked through within the first hour as the rain pounds away on my parka and pack cover. At least it brings out the lush spring colors:

Twelve miles in hard rain.
The green leaves wetly vivid,
the wet red earth.

This close to Springer the Trail is choked with hikers, many half clueless, afraid of hypothermia because they haven't brought the right gear for this cool, dank weather. Some, without rain jackets or packcovers or even tents, just squat in the shelters, which fill by mid-afternoon. And yet—the pines, the roots and rocks, the birds singing whenever the rain lets up a bit, the evergreen shrubs all feel like home by now.

Wild pink azaleas
welcome me home to the trail.
The long hike begins.

Gooch Mountain shelter fills to overflowing—even the narrow space under the picnic table harbors a big wet Labrador retriever. First up and eager to leave the crowd, I cook breakfast as quietly as I can, using the red light option on my headlamp to cause less glare.

Cooking in red light,
the food looks strange by headlamp.
It tastes just the same.

The rain temporarily softens to a heavy mist, through which I climb over a series of low mountains: Ramrock, Big Cedar, Granny Top.

I see less, and that
less is muted, intimate.
Walking in the clouds.

The trail grows wilder, rockier, and wetter as it heads north, with fantastically cascading streams running directly across it:

A cascading stream,
triple branched and pristine. But I've
just drunk from the spring.

No worries about dehydration on this hike, though I begin to wonder how much longer my feet can stay this wet before they start to blister.

By the time I'm making the climb up to the summit of Blood Mountain one little toe has ripped open and I'm badly in need of a second wind. And at that moment, the trail rising above 4000 feet for the first time, a turn in the path opens up a view of dozens of rhododendrons in full bloom, succeeded by bright flame azaleas running from orange to red-orange to red. The rain lightens again for a bit and I hear the first thrushes singing and the first towhees making their signature call, which I try to hear as it is and not as I've learned to identify it.

Listening to towhees,
trying to hear—trying ***not***
to hear "drink your tea."

I stop in the late afternoon at the Walasi-Yi center in Neel's Gap to pick up my first maildrop and decide to stay in the bunkhouse to avoid a rainstorm. The next morning the skies clear for awhile as I begin an 18 mile day of Georgia ups and downs, my right little toe hurting so much that at times that I feel nauseous. Still, I manage to relish the privilege of hiking day after day in the southern Appalachians.

The first wild iris—
twin-stemmed, rooted in the mud.
Friendly reminder.

Today I hike up Levelland Mountain, Wolf Laurel Top, Cowrock Mountain, Wildcat Mountain, Poor Mountain, Sheep Rock Top, Rocky Knob, and Blue Mountain, among others, and down into notches with names like Wide Gap, Low Gap, and Red Clay Gap.

Go up the mountain,
then head down to the next gap.
Repeat many times.

On Wildcat Mountain an indigo bunting stands out brightly against the pine trees. Then, part way into the gentle descent into Low Gap, a smallish bear runs across the trail a hundred yards ahead of me.

Crash. The young bear darts
across the trail, moving fast
as I keep moving.

Forty-five minutes later another thunderstorm hits and my boots, carefully dried out overnight at the Walasi-Yi Center, soak through within minutes. By now my little toe has opened up like a split grape. But I can still walk. Alone at Blue Mountain shelter at 7 p.m. I marvel at how the crowds have thinned out, the greenhorns still squatting out the rain further south, the weekenders all gone home (according to my Trail journal, it's Tuesday). Then at 9, when I'm already asleep, in crashes a friendly, noisy hiker, Go Slow, banging his pots around as he cooks, snoring loudly as soon as he falls asleep. I like him, though—his heartiness, his lack of self-consciousness.

After two nights of fitful sleep and with another day of ups and downs ahead of me I start to flag, worrying too that my toe will become infected. But the skies clear early with a broad lake of mist below in the Gap.

The sun is waiting
above the misty valley.
Raindrops stop dripping.

This day I pass almost no one on the trail, just a few dayhikers late in the afternoon. So the constant labor of the spiders and inchworms is all for me to undo.

Silk threads span the trail.
I break through dozens, hundreds.
First one out today.

I stop for lunch on top of Tray Mountain, nearly 5000 feet high, covered with vivid, bright pink rhododendrons that make me think of a woman I've been spending time with back home, though in general I'm much too tired on my long hikes to feel anything like erotic craving.

No desire out here.
Yet I see her in lush pink
rhododendron blooms.

I spend the night at woodsy Deep Gap Shelter and for once enjoy complete solitude, not even a mouse to trouble it, sleeping deeply until a wood thrush awakens me early the next morning.

A mile or two out of Deep Gap I startle a large male wild turkey on the trail—he lurches awkwardly into a low flight and hits tree branch after tree branch as he struggles to gain altitude. The little toe feels a bit better at first, the trail smooth, eminently walkable hard red Georgia dirt for long stretches, then occasional rocks, then all rocks for a time, reminiscent of New Hampshire. Leaving Georgia I look back on the country I've hiked through from a viewpoint just shy of the North Carolina border. From this as from nearly every highpoint, you see cluster after cluster of similarly low, densely forested mountains—why does the Trail go through this range and no other?

In this wide country
of mountain ranges, just one
to follow northbound.

From here on until my end point north of Davenport Gap, 250 miles from Amicalola Falls, the Trail hovers between North Carolina and Tennessee, the transitions unmarked, a green zone that knows nothing of borders.

I camp at Muskrat Creek with a dozen hikers—I'm back in a "bubble" of northbounders—and leave early for a big day, nineteen miles and at least 2500 feet of elevation gain. My toe is raging again—I hike in searing pain at times, limping, rebandage at the first shelter I come to, and the pain levels out some. I walk with the pain as with a mantra or a koan—"what is this?"—"who is the one that keeps walking?"

A nineteen mile day
with a toe burst like a grape.
Who is there to mind?

And the day has its pleasures, like all days on the Trail, fewer ups and downs, longer ridge walks as in the Whites or even in the Northwest, hours and hours hiking above 4000 feet.

Exhilarating—
so high on this ridge, while still
treading solid earth.

At times, for as much as half an hour at a stretch, the pain stops, almost as though the pain signals from my toe have given up, but I desperately wish for dry socks and boots so it can heal a bit. As it has every day rain threatens and I struggle not to take it too personally, not to find myself absurdly arguing with the weather—

> *"No more rainstorms, please.*
> *I need my boots to dry out."*
> *Low thunder replies.*

I grow dependent on my walking stick, the same hardwood branch I found beside the trail four years back, the one I used to fend off the feisty peregrine falcon crossing the Susquehanna the year before. There's no way I could forget it and leave it behind now at a rest top or campsite—the stick has become practically as much "me" as an arm or leg.

> *If my walking stick*
> *of four hundred miles is now*
> *me, then what am I?*

Maybe nothing. Maybe everything. The long high ridges look out over a broad band of green, forested hills and mountains, their outlines softened by the mist. There's a rock scramble up Albert Mountain with its fire tower, then a quick half mile to Big Spring shelter where, for once, I arrive just ahead of the late afternoon rain.

The next day the Trail gradually descends nine miles through mountain laurel corridors and rhododendron tunnels to Winding Stair Gap, where I need to find a ride into Franklin, NC, my first and only town stop. More Trail magic: as I make my way into the parking area, I see a young hiker with a bandaged knee just pulling her backpack out of a car. I ask the driver, a middle-aged woman, if she can give me a ride back into Franklin. It turns out that she is a "Trail Angel," a local Samaritan who helps distance hikers, the first I've ever met in a parking area, on the very day I most need one. She agrees to take me to a pharmacy on the way to my motel and I stock up on Benadryl (I'm also suffering from poison ivy), gauze, alcohol pads, Tough Strip band aids, and more ibuprofen (lots more). I decide to "zero" in Franklin the next day as well, with my foot up, my toe uncovered, and lots of dry air. I would need still another day for anything like full healing, but after forty hours of rest the toe closes up enough that I can go on with far less pain.

So a day later, now resigned to hiking at a two mile per hour amble, with extra time for rests and elevation gain, I climb back out of the gap.

The town drops away
as I ascend Siler Bald—
birdsong and truck sounds.

Ash has been telling me about his new book, which argues that efforts to protect and heal the natural world have been hampered by the notion of "nature" itself—as something separate from us and from where we ordinarily find ourselves, as something we need to go to rather than find all around us in window gardens and median strips, growing from cracks in the sidewalk and in the bathroom caulking and in us. So this morning I follow Ash in celebrating the "urbanatural" rather than making the truck engines, as they shift to lower gears, something out of place. A practice entirely in keeping with Buddhist notions of emptiness, as Ash well knows. Yet I do feel distinctly happy and excited to go back to the woods, the rhododendrons, the mountain laurels, the warblers and thrushes and woodpeckers, the ridges and hills and gaps, the earth and herb and flower smells, and, now, a series of grassy balds to climb—as the *Heart Sutra* reminds us, "emptiness is also form." We need to keep protecting and, whenever possible, adding to this rare green corridor running from Springer to Katahdin even while we fully accept the noise of the jet flying overhead and acknowledge the car and the fuel and the highway system that bring us to the Trail, not to mention all the "unnatural" work of maintaining that keeps us walking it.

For some reason I see more snails on the trail today than ever before. I notice how vulnerable they are despite their hard shells, so thin and delicate, and their vulnerability touches me, perhaps because I've been so aware of my own vulnerability over the past few days.

My foot still tender,
I swing my boot high over
each snail in the path.

Sixteen miles and nine hours after leaving Winding Stair Gap, sitting on the edge of Cold Spring shelter, I read a series of increasingly frantic entries in the Trail register. Three out of the past four nights hikers have had their food stolen by a nuisance bear. The last entry approaches hysteria—a young distance hiker I remember from a few night earlier writes how the bear actually followed him around the campsite as he hung his food and then, in a fit of desperation, threw his toothpaste into the privy. In the dark, he claims, the bear began climbing into the shelter. Too tired to move on, I cook dinner quickly and hang my foodsack far from the shelter and as cleverly as I can manage, using extra loops and knots. For once I hope for shelter mates, preferably a nice couple with a large dog or two, and of course this turns out to be one of those coveted solitary nights. I've been reading a book by the Zen teacher Taizan Maezumi and, by chance, tonight's dharma talk happens to be on the concept of "no-fear." I fall asleep waiting for the bear and wake up with a start when I hear scratching near my head—only an inquisitive deer mouse. I wake up once more when the bear finally comes looking for my food—I can hear him snuffling the air—and somehow fall asleep again when he goes off in search of it.

Alone with a bear
last night's practice was "no-fear."
The results were mixed.

In the morning my bearbag still hangs intact from its high branch, though a smaller branch near it has been freshly snapped off.

I've been out for ten days now, including the rest day in Franklin, and my usual sense of self has started to erode, something many distance hikers experience but maybe intensified in my case by five years of daily Zen practice. Another big day starts, eighteen and a half miles to go and 4000 feet to climb, 3000 of them in one long stretch out of the Nantahala Gorge. Hard, very hard at times, yet somehow doable. But *who* is doing this?

Who is this hiker,
these feet that keep on plodding,
eyes that never tire?

Flowers line the trail, the evergreen shrubs still in bloom, and a dark brown ground skink slithers by, snake like with its shiny skin, tiny legs, and long tail. A family of wild turkeys bursts noisily out of the bushes on top of a ridge, crashing their way down the slope, and a yellowthroat, a tiny warbler with a bright yellow breast and black-masked face, flits across a creek. Plunging down toward the Gorge the trail enters a damp, shaded zone of Spanish moss and lichen covered rocks, then climbs up through trees studded with exotic looking fungi, oyster mushrooms and wood ears and artist's conks. I'd seen a solitary orchid, then a small stand of pink lady slippers a day or two before, and for a moment I think I've finally spotted an elusive yellow lady slipper. No—a curled up yellow leaf.

I have never seen
a yellow lady slipper.
So I keep looking.

The NOC (Natanhala Outdoor Center) in the Gorge reminds me of Mount Washington—too many tourists, cars, cameras—so I pass up the chance to stop in for a beer. This ends up saving me from a major soaking when a heavy thunder shower hits two minutes after I dart into the big new shelter at Sassafras Gap, running the last tenth of a mile through the storm's first sprinkles.

Climbing out of high Sassafras Gap the trail pushes above 5000 feet as it ascends Cheoah Bald. North of the Natanhala the forest has changed—mistier (this must be the weather rising out of the Gorge), more pine, Spanish moss, and mountain laurel bushes making long, shady channels out of trail sections.

Hiking in the mist:
Spanish moss, laurel tunnels,
petals underfoot.

Hundreds of brilliant orange flame azaleas dot the hillsides, the blossoms piercing through the mist like torchlights.

Softening all else,
the mist can't dim the brightness
of flame azaleas.

Then the long descent toward Fontana Dam, more than 3000 feet below the line of high balds (Siler, Wayah, Copper Ridge, Wesser, Swim) that ends with Cheoah. I stop for lunch at Brown Fork Gap shelter where an ovenbird, ordinarily shy, pecks at the ground in front of my feet, showing off its bright black eyes ringed with white, its darkly speckled breast, and its dramatic crown, a bold yellow-orange stripe between dark brown borders.

Much heard, seen just once—
tiny, speckle-breasted, eyes
large and dark and bright.

I stay the night at the next shelter I come to, Cable Gap, arriving early enough to rest my feet and legs, rub Benadryl cream into my ever-larger poison ivy rash (my sleeping bag must be contaminated), and hang my food bag as high as I can, wanting the bears to stay as wild as possible for my sake and for theirs.

A short morning's walk, just five miles or so, takes me to Fontana Dam and a shuttle to the Fontana Village Resort, where a maildrop, a room in the lodge, and a beer and a shower wait for me. I spend the afternoon airing out my little toe (my feet are otherwise blister free, which makes my Achilles toe all the more frustrating) and scrubbing out the inside of my sleeping bag. Pretty and pricey, the resort is a splurge, one I'm more than happy to spring for—I would extend the stay another night for the sake of my toe if it weren't all booked up. The next day, Friday, begins the long Memorial Day weekend and the last five days of my hike, which will take me into the heart of the Great Smoky Mountains.

Talking with northbound thruhikers on dozens of my hikes to date, by now in every Trail state from North Carolina to Maine, hardly anyone ever mentioned the Smokies as a highlight of the AT. I have no idea why. The section through the Great Smoky Mountains is one of the most gorgeous and dramatic of the entire Trail. A haven for bear, elk, and many smaller critters, protected from logging and hunting, it also counts as one of the wildest, despite the proximity to (and occasional crossing through) major tourist spots. The sense of adventure starts right away with 4000 feet of hard climbing to get from Fontana Dam to the top of Little Bald, where the Trail rises above 5000 feet again. For several days of hiking to come the Trail stays above 4400 feet, much of the time above 5000, and frequently topping 6000. The Smoky Mountains famously have their own weather system, the mist and cloud cover that gives them their name, and a unique ecosystem as a result though, ironically, my five days up in the heights turn out to be the sunniest overall of the seventeen days I spend on the Trail.

Hiking up a series of long switchbacks the most striking change, at first, has to do with the quiet of the woods—far from roads, hikers widely spread and in small groups, the only noise the singing of warblers and the hum of insects. At one point I think I hear raindrops falling around me, though I feel nothing and only a few clouds drift overhead. Then I look down to see the ground moving with little creatures striped with green and black and yellow bands.

Hundreds of crickets
jump ahead of my boot steps,
pattering like rain.

All that day I find myself noticing insects, and not just the flies beginning to bite me. Scenes that could have been atmospheric shots in a horror movie instead strike me as manifesting their own, indifferent beauty:

Black round dung beetles
jostle for space on bear scat
with blue-tailed butterflies.

Hiking out of Russell Field early the next morning I find the trail lined with hundreds of little bluets.

These simple bluets,
low growing, four-petalled, pale,
complete the sunrise.

Today the trail stays high, going over Rocky Top (5455 feet), Cold Spring Knob (5240) and Silers Bald (5618); even the shelter at Double Spring Gap, where I stay the night, stands at a height of over 5500 feet. Walking along the top of the world I take my time, savoring the last few days of the hike, stopping wherever stopping seems good, allowing myself ten hours to cover sixteen and a half miles. This day takes me from the hardwood forest of maple, birch, and flame azalea up to a region of towering spruce and fir, the evergreens growing taller than most anywhere else I've been in the Eastern Forest. Something is changing.

A coyote howls at 4 a.m. but I lull myself back to sleep, with only fourteen miles to cover. And as the trail reaches new heights climbing Mount Buckley (6582 feet), I realize why the evergreens have gotten so big and why the terrain here looks so oddly familiar. I'm hiking through a temperate rain forest, the eastern counterpart to the Olympic National Forest back in my home state. Lush ferns sprout up everywhere, decaying trees left unmolested to enrich the forest floor are covered with mosses and fungi, the standing evergreens soar overhead. I half expect to see a whistling marmot or a mountain goat; instead two white-tailed bucks, much larger than the stunted ones I've seen from the Shenandoahs to New England, stand in the trail ahead of me before grudgingly moving away.

Just before the climb up Mount Buckley the trail fills with an insect I've never seen before, bizarre and unearthly, small bodied with a single large, luminous wing glowing in the morning sunlight. Then, closer up, I see them for what they are: flies carrying large, transparent egg sacs.

Small flies half-floating
with egg sacs like silk lanterns,
pale and translucent.

The rain forest keeps bringing thoughts of Dad and I think of how much he would have loved the Smokies, and also, perhaps, how pointless he would have found it to travel here when the Olympics were only a few hours from home. So I walk them for both of us. In the year since Dad's death he has been more, not less, present to me on my solitary hikes. Not as a ghostly presence, haunting me, but not as a mere idea or set of memories either. I hear his voice rather than imagine what he would say; I see through his eyes rather than think, "Dad would love this." I'm channeling him, or the parts of him that he passed on to me over our years of hikes and camping trips. I'm living on my inheritance.

And the trail continues to climb till it reaches Clingman's Dome, the highest point, at 6643 feet, on the entire Appalachian Trail. A little disappointing, despite long, spectacular views from the observation tower on top, since a road leads nearly to the summit and all sense of wilderness must be left behind for a time as you enter a tourist zone. A feeling that only intensifies a few hours later at Newfound Gap, a highway crossing at just over 5000 feet (even the gaps here are high), as hordes of day visitors eat their lunches, snap pictures, and debate on whether to hazard the few miles to Charlie's Bunion and back. But by nightfall the crowds have disappeared again and the shelter at Icewater Spring is only half full. The open front looks out on miles of picturesque green hills to the east and south and wood thrushes sing in the half-light. The next morning, leaving the shelter in the mist, I have Charlies's Bunion all to myself.

On this, my last full day in the woods, I don't see another soul over the first ten miles of walking. I do see a number of juncos, as I have each day in the Park. They have a trick here I'd never noticed before, nestling under leaves just next to or even directly on the trail and then fluttering up without warning as you pass. This morning a tiny juvenile flutters up half comically.

A fledgling junco
starts up inches from my boot,
trusting to new wings.

All morning a stiff wind ruffles the tops of the tall evergreens, making me wonder about a return of the rain and not really minding any more if it does return. So far all the blowing leads only to a few sprinkles.

This morning's hard wind
seems to portend no more than
another good day.

The trail follows long ridges over rocks, skirting big moss-covered downed trees, still in the rain forest, with mist blowing in to complete the effect. Every day has been a good day. I both do and do not want this long walk to end.

The final day of hiking, eighteen miles from TriCorner Knob to Davenport Gap and a bit beyond to Standing Bear Farm, takes me down nearly five thousand feet, though this being the Smokies it also includes some lovely ridge walking and as much as two thousand feet of ups. I move briskly through mist and cloud, giving myself to the walking, not thinking about the days ahead, not yet certain where I'll sleep tonight or whether I'll stop again at Creekside or power through to Boston the next day. The clouds drift apart at times and dramatic ridge views open up revealing high peaks in swirling mist, the great smoky mountains indeed. Fir and spruce give place to hemlocks and large swathes of rhododendron, still in bloom, harboring at least four kinds of thrush: veery, hermit, Swainson's, and wood thrush. Wild turkeys, dark-eyed juncos, grey squirrels, and eastern chipmunks dart in and out of passing light rains, fresh bear scat on the path hints at all the creatures hidden in the brush, keeping away, staying wild. The skies open up again, the mountaintops rise once more over mist, and then the trail dips sharply down into the Gap and the peaks disappear from view.

SUMMER

The water is clear all the way down. Nothing ever polished it.
That is the way it is.

Keizan Jokin, *Denkōroku*

July 2005. The hike starts out well, certainly better than our last hike, to October Mountain, when we stepped out of the car into a surprise foot of snow. Leaving the Housatonic near Falls River, the first half mile or so of walking gives Lida a nice taste of the Trail through Connecticut: the river, the unkempt pastures, the rural woodland feel. Lida spots a tiny shrew running across the path and then points upward to a turkey vulture high overhead tilting on the air currents, its wings held in a flattened V shape. Bursts of hauntingly beautiful birdsong come to us from the brush and I tell Lida that this is the music of the wood thrush, our American nightingale. (Though neither of us has ever heard a nightingale.) Together we watch a frog spotted like a leopard hop alongside the trail lined with wild geraniums, star moss, and mountain laurels, some still in bloom.

Then the terrain rises dramatically in front of us along with the temperature.

With only 700 vertical feet to ascend no one could call this a major climb, but for Lida, still only ten, it proves forbidding enough. Not so much the elevation gain as the combination of that and the full heat of day, rising well into the 80s here on the exposed flank of Sharon Mountain. All the considerable toughness my daughter showed on the hike back from October Mountain a few months earlier, five miles in a light but steady rain through slushy snow, seems to evaporate in the searing heat. Flushed and uncomfortable in her boots—I wonder silently if I accidentally warped them in drying them by the campfire back on our snow hike—Lida calls for rests again and again, and then can barely get herself restarted. I offer just as often to take her backpack, a half-size version of my own, until at last she grudgingly consents. I barely notice the added weight as I carry it in one hand up the rocks. Soon we find a shady spot under a granite crag not much more than halfway up. We stop for lunch.

Lida wants to go back. I start bargaining. I had intended for us to go to the Pine Swamp Brook lean-to, overlapping one of my earlier hikes and giving us a good six mile day, but I now propose stopping at the Sharon Mountain campsite, less than four miles from our starting point. Besides, the swamp will be full of mosquitoes—better to camp on a nice breezy mountaintop, though as yet there's no sign of a cooling breeze. Lida balks: the trail ahead of us looks endlessly steep from here. I pass her the m&m's and hope for a burst of energy. It doesn't come.

We keep debating until a solo dayhiker comes in view, picking his way down the mountainside. Lida asks him how far to the top, a question I try never to ask. He tells us, wrongly as it turns out, maybe another ten, fifteen minutes. Lida agrees to try it. More than half an hour later, we see the ridgeline just above us, shaded by evergreens, and the long crisis passes. We're ready to have fun again.

Lida reclaims her backpack and we walk the ridge together, two buddies out for an overnight. The heat lessens under the tree cover and a steady breeze does magically start up. Best of all, as we near the campsite, my eyes pick up a flash of bright orange in the leafcover just off the trail. It's a red eft, one of my favorite of all woodland creatures, and I can't wait to show it to my daughter. She bends down for a better look and is instantly entranced, as anyone would be. In addition to its glowing red orange color and its side rows of red spots, ringed with black like so many round eyes, it looks remarkably, invitingly, almost painfully delicate. With its lithe three-inch body and whiplike tail, most of all with its slender, sensitive looking toes, four on the front legs, five on the back, like the hands of a fetus, it goes straight to her heart.

And unlike the tiny lizard it resembles it doesn't run. Trusting to its orange color, a blatant warning to crows and foxes of its toxic skin, it just basks. This appearance of trustingness coupled with its friendly looking face, eyes that seem to wink, and a mouthline like a slow smile, makes it even more loveable. Each of us in turn reaches down, extends a careful forefinger, and gives it the gentlest stroke along the spine. And then we move on.

I talk a little about the odd lifecycle of this wonderful critter, trying not to sound too professorly. It starts out in a pond as a sort of tadpole, breathing through gills, looking more as it grows like the salamander it is. Then one day it starts to morph: the tail thins out, the feet begin to look more like hands, and even its color changes from that of a ripe green olive to the fiery color we've just been admiring. It moves from water to land, changes gills for lungs, and lives in the woods that way for up to a few years as an eft. Until it transforms again, now returning to the water as a dark green newt, its tail broad and vertically flattened like an eel's, its skin wet and slimy, its toes thickened, its underside sprinkled with black spots. Only the red spots along the sides of its body remain from its eft phase, giving it its adult name, the red-spotted newt. Lida listens to all this politely enough. Or, more likely, she's making up a story in her head about the eft, not efts in general but the one we've just seen, certain to be a better story than any I could invent for her.

Soon we reach the primitive Sharon Mountain campsite, no shelter, water from a brook, not even a real privy, just a dank, unsheltered wooden seat over a pit out in the woods. (Lida decides she prefers the bushes.) The campsite stays empty except for a few efts that Lida visits with while I set up our big two-person backpacking tent and hang a bearline. We make dinner and then, in the early dusk, watch fireflies blink on and off at the edge of the trees. As though the fireflies have attracted it, lightning begins to flash in the sky. I rush to hang our foodbag and dive after Lida into the tent just as the summer storm begins. We stretch out on our sleeping bags, take out the paperbacks each of us has brought, and read together by headlamp. Rain drums on the tent but not a drop of water comes through the fly. Thunder rumbles, the rain gets even harder, and the inside of the tent, dimly lit by our headlamps, feels like a wolf den, a rabbit burrow, a panther cave. I ask Lida if she's doing OK. She turns to smile at me. "This is great, Dad." The tent keeps us dry. The rain keeps us cool.

The storm passes and by morning the skies have cleared up again. I wake early, retrieve the bear bag, and set up the canister stove. Perched on a damp fallen log next to a wood ear fungus, I sip my espresso-laced hot chocolate and enjoy the cool of the morning woods. I want us to get well down the sunny ridge slope before the heat of day, but I'm not sure how I'll manage to get Lida to leave her sleeping bag any time soon. My kids have already reached the age when, instead of desperately wishing they would go back to sleep for just another thirty minutes, I now have to struggle to get them out of bed at a reasonable hour. As sleepers they're both precocious teenagers, while the years of tending to small children have left me chronically unable to sleep past seven.

Then I notice them. All around the edges of our campsite, empty except for us, my eyes pick out little slashes of orange. The rain has lured dozens and dozens of red efts into the clearing. I've never seen or even imagined seeing so many. Most of them cluster in groups though a few have found their own solitary patch of wet ground to forage. They vary in size, some no longer than Lida's thumb, others as long as my own index finger, and in color—from the dusty orange of a tangerine skin to the lush red-orange of a hazy sunset. Each time I look their numbers seem to have grown.

I open the tentfly and say, loudly as I dare, "Lida, get up! There are about a hundred of those orange salamanders all around the campsite!" She jerks herself awake and I leave her in privacy to get into her camp clothes. She's out within minutes and I point her to the nearest group of efts. While I make us a breakfast of instant oatmeal and hot chocolate, Lida moves around the edges of the clearing, bending over the red efts, studying them, choosing favorites and giving them names. I don't need to tell her not to poke at them or pick them up. She has an innate ability, almost uncanny at times, to enter into the wants and needs and feelings of animals. When she was only four I teasingly accused her of hypnotizing our new kitten—really it was more of a mind meld and the two became permanently bonded. If she put a newt in her hand, it would mean she somehow knew the newt wanted her to.

I pack us up and we head back along the ridge after Lida says her goodbyes. We scamper down the steep ridgeside and bottom out well before noon. As we walk through the fields back toward the Housatonic Lida reaches up to a branch heavy with dark, cylindrical berries and puts one into her mouth. "Lida, do you even know what those are?" I ask her, a little concerned. She looks at me quizzically and tells me, hardly believing I need to be told, that we're standing under a mulberry tree. Something she must have learned in Girl Scouts. It's an eastern berry I never would have encountered in my western childhood and I'm struck for a moment at how my children are native New Englanders in a way I can never be. The mulberries are delicious. And there are many more mulberry trees stretched in front of us.

Soon we're in a wilderness of berries, red and black mulberries hanging overhead, red raspberry bushes closer to the ground and, mingled in with them, another plant I've never seen before, black raspberries. I find an empty plastic bag left over from our early lunch and we fill it with an assortment of berries to bring home to the woman I now call, to myself, Nate and Lida's mother, although she will still be my wife for over a year to come. I know just how pleased she will be by our gesture, can already see her bright, tight smile when we give her this gift from the woods. Once the Ziploc bag has been carefully placed inside my backpack we return to picking berries for ourselves. We work the bushes a few feet apart, moving in tandem, a bear and its cub. So ripe they drop into our purple-stained hands, the mulberries and the red and black raspberries burst into sweet, tangy juice as we pop them into our mouths. We eat them singly and we experiment with various combinations, red and black, red and red, black and black. We take our time. We eat wild berries to our hearts' content.

August 2005. We've been watching the grouse for over a minute when the little girl comes into view, closely followed by her parents. I stop them with a raised hand, put my finger over my lips, and then gesture toward the bird, which stands its ground a yard or two away from us. At first the girl doesn't see it—she's puzzled, unsure of what's happening—so Nate goes to her, crouches down to her level, and points until her face brightens, her eyes grow wide, her smile flashes out. In a soft voice, Nate introduces her to the exotic looking mountain creature in front of us. We had seen one the day before as well, on the Garfield Ridge. So his words sound familiar, versions of my own. He tells her its name, the spruce grouse, and how its other name, the foolhen, comes from its lack of fear of humans, so unusual in such a wild creature. How she can tell it's a male from the bright red comb over its eye and the black on its throat and breast, with the black and white stripes on the sides. He tells her about the whirring noise it made low in its throat when we first saw it—she wishes it would start whirring again. And when she starts to move impulsively toward it he stops her wordlessly with the lightest of touches.

I glance quickly toward the mother and feel relieved to find her almost as charmed as her daughter obviously is by this tall, handsome boy. And my own heart starts filling, with love for him, with gratitude that we can have this experience together, with pride. I feel proud of how gently he takes the young girl in hand, powerfully reminded of how gentle he used to be with Lida and will be again, I'm certain, when the early storms of adolescence have passed. I'm proud that at thirteen he can handle these rugged ridge trails high in the White Mountains, despite his many claims otherwise. And I'm proud of strengths he has that never came to me, not just his sheer height (due to surpass mine soon enough) but his lack of shyness, his extroverted, even magnetic ways. The fool hen finally moves off and we continue down the ridge, quickly leaving the young family behind.

Once out of earshot I tell Nate how much I appreciated what just happened, the way he helped the girl take in the sheer wonder of the spruce grouse, giving her a quiet lesson in how to appreciate wild things. I tell him, my voice almost catching, that the feeling he had just now, of pleasure in her pleasure, in passing on his own love and knowledge of the mountains and mountain creatures, is something I've felt many times with him, on our dayhikes and now on our backpacking trip. Nate looks at me with flat eyes and he flattens his voice too as he says, "I didn't feel anything like that, Dad. I just told her what the bird was called. I don't even know what you're talking about." We hike on in silence.

Our trip, five days in the White Mountains, going from one Appalachian Mountain Club "high hut" to the next, started out well enough. We left the car in Lafayette Campground, just off I-93, and did the easy backpack up to Lonesome Lake Hut. Switching to small, compressible daypacks, we climbed Cannon Mountain together, once on the AT but no longer, the first of ten 4000 footers on our trip agenda. From the summit we could look east across the notch to the Franconia Ridge and the series of mountains we would climb the next day, as well as south to the Kinsman Ridge and Moosilauke. Then a quick scramble back down to the hut in time for a plunge in Lonesome Lake before dinner. The water is cool and brackish, perfect for a quick swim. On our way to the main hut building for dinner we find a snowshoe hare in its brown summer coat nibbling grass right in front of the porch, a crowd of kids clustered around watching it.

Day two does not go nearly so well. We get a late start after a huge Hut breakfast, pancakes and sausage and scrambled eggs and juice, and catch our trail at the south end of the lake. There's a perfectly reasonable way to hike with a thirteen year old from Lonesome Lake to Greenleaf Hut: head back down to the Lafayette Campground, cross the highway, and hike up the Bridle Path Trail. But that does not fit my plan, which is to backpack at least part of the Appalachian Trail with Nate. So instead we take the Cascade Brook Trail (the local trail names have long survived their incorporation into the AT), rugged and rocky, mossy with stream crossings and dank dells carved into the mountainside, still mostly shaded by the massive ridge to the east. We descend some 900 feet, tunnel under I-93, and then head up, up, remorselessly up the Liberty Springs Trail toward the Franconia Ridge almost 3000 feet above us. (By the end of the day, we'll gain at least 4000 feet in all.) By now the sun has cleared the ridge and the temperature quickly rises into the low 80s. We climb from rock group to rock group, sometimes using our hands to negotiate an especially tricky granite outcropping. Soon Nate is calling for a rest every minute or so. I just want to get to the ridge—my own hiking style is to keep moving, promising myself I'll rest at the top, which I often then fail to do, since once at the top the hiking gets easier. This clearly is not going to work for my son.

I negotiate a deal with him: every five minutes we will stop for one minute. Nate grudgingly agrees the way someone agrees when they know they are getting the worse end. This works, for a while. Other hikers pass us in both directions, including a woman in her mid-sixties resolutely making her way down the rocks with two Leki poles, one good leg, and one leg half made of what looks like titanium. I give Nate a pointed glance but he does not seem to register any implied contrast—as soon as she moves out of earshot he starts moaning again. "*Dad*, isn't it five minutes *yet*?"

"It's been two minutes."

"Urrrrrr!"

The climb feels endless, especially with all the stops, which I spend balanced on my feet, itching to get moving again, while Nate sprawls on the nearest smooth rock. When we start up again he quickly falls behind, so I have to wait a minute or two for him to catch up and then a minute while we rest. I know how important it is to stay positive—we'll never make it through the week otherwise.

Two thirds of the way up, or what I hope is at least two thirds, I've pulled so far ahead of him on one segment that when five minutes are up I just call down to him, "one minute rest!" And keep going. I have a new plan. I double my speed, pushing myself up the sharp incline. Soon I can't hear Nate asking me where I've gone anymore.

There's an AMC campsite at Liberty Springs a few hundred feet below the ridgeline. I reach it, leave my backpack on the platform of the caretaker's fixed tent, and half jog, half slide back down the trail. When I reach Nate, not terribly far from where I had left him, he wants to start an argument. I ignore him and take his backpack. "Now it will be easier," I tell him. "Let's go."

It does get easier. When we reach the campsite we take a long drink from the spring, clear, cold, delicious water pouring from the heart of the rock. We put our backpacks on and, at last, reach the Franconia Ridge Trail. But we don't head north toward Greenleaf because, strange to say, I have yet another challenge for Nate.

The whole return to backpacking wasn't supposed to be about me, not at the beginning. It was supposed to be about Nate and me and, in a few years, Lida. We had been doing family dayhikes from the time the kids could run, but backpacking simply had not occurred to me till, on the top of Mount Juneau one summer, my eyes grew fixated on a perfect camping spot, a dream site, close to the summit. The hike started just a quarter mile from our B&B in town, yet after a after a steep climb it felt to me like a return to the heart of the North Cascades. I looked at that campsite, just big enough for a two-person tent, with such longing that crazy plans to come back that afternoon with a tarp and a blanket started running through my head. Then I looked at Nate, a sturdy eleven year old, his legs and torso molded by years of ballet training, his proportions already close to an adult's. And I thought, I have to start taking this boy into the mountains. Like Dad took me.

From the junction of the Liberty Springs Trail and the Franconia Ridge trail the top of Mount Liberty is only a third of a mile off to the right. And since I also want us to hike all forty-eight of the 4K's together, it seems silly not to go ahead and summit when we're already most of the way up the peak. So I hang Nate's backpack in a dead tree off the trail and we head up. Again freed of the pack, Nate walks easily; we have lunch on the summit where we can look down and see how very far we've climbed. Nate looks down with a mixture of disbelief, annoyance, and grudging pleasure. At least, I think there's a trace of grudging pleasure.

The ridge trail comes as a relief after the slog up the mountainside, but we still have a thousand feet to climb with three peaks—Little Haystack, Lincoln, and Lafayette—between us and the descent to the hut. A slight breeze keeps off any mosquitoes that might have followed us up from the notch, though nothing like the blast of wind that literally knocked me off my feet the last time we hiked the Ridge. The breeze keeps off the bugs but not the heat. Nate grows red-faced again on the climb up Little Haystack, which starts to feel like the Liberty Trail all over again. Finally I offer to take his backpack once more—as it turns out, for the last time. Nate bounds ahead and moments later the trail jags to become a tough scramble up steep, nearly featureless granite. Too proud to call Nate back, I make my way up by throwing his pack ahead of me, scrambling and then catching it on its slide back down. Soon we've summited again and Nate relaxes as he sees the top of Lafayette less than two miles away. We hike on with no further grumbling, though by now we're both pushing our limits. A hiker passing us from the north looks hard at our faces and asks, "Are you two O.K.? Do you need water?" I wave him off and we stumble ahead.

At last we drop down to the hut, well in time for dinner, and Nate meets a trio of lively girls a year or two older than he is. He soon has them giggling and by mid-evening the threesome has become a foursome. Their families are doing the same traverse so Nate will meet up with them at the next two huts to come. Which either makes him less happy than I would have thought or more happy than he's willing to let on. The start of the next day, from Greenleaf to Galehead, involves the thousand foot climb back up to the top of Lafayette ("Dad, I can't believe we have to climb this *again!*") with another 1700 feet spread over the rest of the hike. Before we leave I take a few pounds of gear from Nate's pack and put it into mine. That seems to help.

Although we stay above 3000 feet all day, the downs on the ridgeline still feel hard, steep, and rocky, and the ups are just as steep—more cajoling and bargaining. But the mountains offer plenty of distractions. On the long ascent up Mount Garfield (our fifth 4K of the trip at 4488 feet) we pass stands of blue-bead lily, with clusters of big, poisonous berries the color of blueberries on tall, vertical stalks, and more Indian pipe than I've seen in one place before. Also known as the corpse plant, these are pale white, ghostlike stalks ending in a bell shaped flower than hangs down limply—for some reason, we both have a liking for this strange plant. Nate points out a leopard-spotted pickerel frog and soon after a toad hops across our path. We come up on a male foolhen that spends five full minutes walking up the trail with us—this gets Nate smiling openly for once. We watch another snowshoe hare bounding through the trees below the ridge. For the most part we walk in silence.

Scrambling up Garfield summit, an imposing jumble of rocks, I wish again that Nate were having more fun. I want him to realize how strong he is, to tap into the reserves of stamina I know he has—not so much to toughen up as to meet the toughness already inside him. I think a lot about how driven my own usual hiking style is—in part because on this trip I'm forced to hold back—and I think back to when I was ten or eleven, younger than Nate is now. It was my first summer hiking with the Boy Scouts. I was one of the youngest and also one of the smallest in the group—what growth I got came late. I soon realized that as the little guy I had two options. I could be the weenie little guy and hang back with the slowest of the dads and the pudgiest, sweatiest of the kids, letting all the other boys outstrip me. Or I could be the tough little guy, the one who keeps surprising everyone by somehow keeping pace with the bigger kids, the athletic ones. The ones who looked like Nate.

I chose the way of toughness. I somehow caught onto the fact that the difference between being skinny and being wiry was mainly attitude and the ability to suck up pain. I lengthened my stride to keep up with longer legs. I hustled, taking ten steps for a bigger kid's eight. Over that summer and the next, I doggedly moved up from the third knot of kids to the second, edging into the space between the second and the first, the oldest and coolest boys, not daring to challenge them yet. And I made for myself an ironclad rule, a dark imperative that no one else could know about, not Dad, not Brian, not my best friend: I would never, ever, ever be the one to call for a rest. My calves could be cramping, my lungs burning, my temples pounding, I could be using every single brain cell not needed to put one foot in front of the other to will, by some desperate stab at telepathy, another kid, any other kid, to sigh, throw in the towel, and plump his butt down on the nearest rock. And then, sometimes not until I'd neared the point of vomiting over the ridge side, it would happen. I would take a few more steps up the switchback, turn around, and look a little surprised to find everyone else beginning to sit down. And then I would join them, amazed that I had pulled it off again, that I was still, against all reason, keeping them all fooled.

The haze dissipates, giving us long views from Garfield into the Pemigewasset Wilderness. At the center, green and mysterious, stands Owl's Head, the most remote of the forty-eight 4K's and the only one without an official summit trail. "One day," I say to Nate who, of course, shakes his head. We take our time, averaging about a mile an hour, not a bad pace on this rugged terrain, and despite any complaining Nate stays strong, much stronger than he lets on. We finish the climb up to Galehead Hut by 3:30, choose our bunks and take an hour to rest, and then follow the half-mile trail to Galehead summit, taking only a single daypack with some emergency water. By the time we return to the hut Nate's three friends have arrived and he goes off with them while I talk with some of the other hikers doing the traverse. Before dinner I stealthily point out a sad, defeated looking couple across the common area and tell Nate, in a low voice, that they've decided to bail the next morning; they'll follow a side trail to the highway and then take a private shuttle back to their car rather than going on to the next two huts.

"*We* should bail, Dad," Nate responds, deadly serious.

"Nate, why would we do that? We got here in good time today, the hardest day is behind us, and you're doing great, I didn't want us to go any faster today than we went. And we practically ran up that summit trail. We're in good shape, pal."

"We should *totally* bail."

I manage to get Nate moving by 7:45 the next morning, our best start yet. Right out of the gate we have a steep, rocky 1100 feet to climb up to the top of South Twin, where we sit for awhile watching the cloud shadows and the views come and go as the sun fitfully tries to break through. Then, well above timberline at 4902 feet, we stow Nate's pack up behind a tall granite outcropping, first removing his snack bag to discourage any marauding critters. We follow a spur trail a mile or so to climb North Twin, another bonus 4K at 4751 feet, making eight so far. (Some of the mountains we climb, like Little Haystack, don't "count" because the ridgeline does not descend deeply enough from the nearest official 4K summit: too easy.) In this case we lose almost 250 feet descending into the col, so North Twin meets the odd but fair test of "topographical prominence." This summit, while not much lower than its twin, gives no views, ringed round by gnarled spruce trees, though the ridge in between the two gives us fine views ahead as the sky finally clears. Nate moves easily without his backpack. I've kept mine on, with our snacks and lunches and emergency gear, and toward the end of this side trip I'm panting just a little from the effort to keep up with him. Nate looks back at me pointedly, his eyes sharp: "Are you *OK*, Dad?"

Once back at South Twin the bulk of the climbing is behind us, as we'll lose much more elevation than we gain over our last two days of hiking. Still, the terrain stays rugged, the shorter climbs adding up, the steep downs almost as hard, and Nate soon claims to be struggling again, though to me he looks like a boyish mountain deity. We hike over Mount Guyot and then up Zealand Mountain, a few hundred feet shorter than Guyot at 4261 feet but more "prominent" and therefore our ninth 4K and our third of the day, once we take the short trail off the AT to the viewless, featureless, decidedly anticlimactic summit. The walk down toward Zealand Falls Hut, more woodsy and less rocky than the ridgelines we've been following, brings delayed rewards:

the spruce grouse that Nate introduces to the little girl we meet, and white throated sparrows singing their eerie little two-note song, the second note always repeated and always dissonant, a little flat—the signature call of the high White Mountains.

We reach the hut before three, with plenty of time to splash around in the Zealand Falls, here more horizontal than vertical with large granite slabs to loll on as the cold water flows over and around you. Nate takes two mountain baths, one with me and a second with his three pretty friends, who arrive about an hour after we do. I explore a side trail leading higher up the falls until I find a mossy nook just a few feet back from the water, where I'm surrounded on three sides by evergreens. I break out the half pint flask of bourbon I've smuggled along, a couple of good swigs for each evening on the trail, and add some water from the stream rushing by to help stretch out the last few ounces.

Hidden and alone, steeping in the sound of the torrent and the smell of the balsam firs, I start reflecting on the last few days with Nate, but find myself instead thinking about the last backpacking trip I ever took with my own father. Brian and I wanted to climb the Brothers, a split peak near the midpoint of the Olympic range, and we had talked Dad into going with us, since he wouldn't let us take the car without him. We brought our neighbor Bucky along to fill out the group. Dad hiked with us up to the base camp, six miles and two thousand vertical feet of gentle switchbacks lined with old growth Douglas firs, passing Lena Lake and following a stream up the Valley of the Silent Men, a mossy rift through the rainforest. We were all happy to be out, though Dad moved slowly. After waiting two hours for him at the tentsite Brian headed back down the trail, returning just before dusk with Dad's pack on his back and Dad shuffling behind.

We started our climb the next morning at first light, leaving Dad to rest up and guard the tents from bears, silver marmots, and mountain goats (we'd had incursions from them all in the Olympics over the years). It was a brutally steep scramble, some 3500 feet to gain over two and a half miles on unmarked paths over scree, boulders, vertical rock and the occasional late snow patch. Brian and I took turns leading while Bucky lagged behind. Though my brother had towered over me for much of our childhood, fully grown we were equals in size and strength, perfect climbing buddies. We challenged each other and looked out for each other and, too often, we pushed each other to take risks. We were not fearless, exactly, but we were closer to fearlessness than we should have been. We had both become hooked on what climbers call "the edge."

This was the climb that nearly killed me. Picking my way down from a false summit on a goat trail over badly rotten rock, crumbling behind me and forcing me to keep going forward when no good way forward presented itself, only an impossible twisting leap kept me from free falling into a jagged gulch a thousand feet below, as my last handhold slid out from the rock face like a smooth peg sliding out from its slot. When I looked down from my landing spot at Brian, who'd found a better descent, there were tears on his face: he had already begun mourning my certain death. He told me I had been smiling grimly, tossing the false handhold behind me into the void as I leaped and spun. (It was not me smiling but the one John Muir calls the "other self"—the ultimate "edge" experience and a story for another time.) We didn't mention any of this to Dad, but we gave up on summiting and bounded down the rocks toward camp as quickly as we could.

Dad had us half packed up by the time we reached the tentsite. It should have been an easy walk back to the car and for three of us it was. But Dad, aging and out of shape, had used everything he had on the way up. After the first mile he admitted he was in pain; by the end of the second mile he admitted he was in trouble. Bucky and I slung his backpack over a hardwood branch and carried it between us down the trail. Brian stayed with Dad, helping him over rocks and guiding him when, his knees repeatedly buckling, he did the last mile or so backwards. When they got to the car Dad's face was less flushed with exertion than pale with anguish and his grey hair looked bleached white, as though we had lured him into aging ten years in a single weekend. Dad never went backpacking with us again.

I can just hear the sound of laughter from downstream, Nate's infectious guffaw impossible to miss against the higher, silvery tones of what sounds like at least half a dozen shrieking girls. Then only stream sounds again. What comes to me now, what hits me for the first time as I think back on that wild expedition, is that Dad must have been fifty years old that year—the age I will turn before two more months have passed.

I add some more water to the little Nalgene flask, nearly losing it in the current, and then sit back to try and sort through all the different emotions suddenly spiking up. Some mix of pride and satisfaction, stopping short of smugness, that at an age when Dad could be hobbled by a twelve mile out and back I could do this White Mountain traverse and only wish we could go faster. Sadness at realizing how far back Dad's decline began and anxiety about how much weaker he will grow now that he can just manage his daily walk around the block. A taste of my own mortality knowing that this midlife renewal of strength and energy will, ultimately, only delay my own certain decline—assuming I live that long. And a surge of compassion mixed with guilt when I think about Nate and what he must be feeling during this trip, outpaced and outdone by the old guy, possibly feeling weaker and more vulnerable instead of, as I had hoped, stronger and tougher for the climbing and scrambling and ridge walking we've just done together. "Dad, *we* should bail."

The skies stay clear all night and when dark falls you can see the entire band of the Milky Way while heat lightning flashes far to the east. In the morning we leave the AT for a leisurely walk down the A to Z Trail to the AMC's Highland Center, where a hot shower, a cold beer for me, and a call to Nate's mom await. En route we take in one last 4K, Mount Tom, off a steep spur trail that annoys Nate to no end. When we reach the summit I raise my arm for a ritual fist bump, as we've done on top of each peak, but Nate leaves me hanging. I don't push it. He's done nearly everything I've asked, and not just over the past four days—only a few weeks ago, on our annual family National Park trip, he and I climbed Hidden Lake Peaks in the North Cascades and Storm King in the Olympics. Storm King was a last minute plan B after Nate refused to cross a fresh, scarily steep rock slide on the approach to Mount Pyramid. It made me miss Brian. I rustle a gallon ziploc out of my backpack and take out a blue pen and the official guide to *The 4000-Footers of the White Mountains*. We find the checklist at the back of the book and fill in the date and our initials, *A & N 8/10/05*, in the blank space on the line that says "Tom 4051 ft. / 1235 m."

Once more the sun burns through the morning fog, as it has each day, and from the top of Mount Tom we get a vivid close-up of Mount Field, lushly green and round like an overturned bowl, a peak we will do on another day, on another trip. But that day never comes. We summit a few more 4Ks together, making twenty in all, yet within a year Nate will have begun refusing to go to the mountains with me any longer, having reached his limit. So I do the other twenty-eight by myself, mostly on fall solo trips but a few in spring and a few in winter on snowshoes. Each time I get home I find the 4,000 footer guide and enter the summit date in pencil. That way, I tell myself, it can be erased and replaced with the real entry in blue ink, when the day comes that I climb it with Nate.

June 2006. As I scan for the white blazes edging the Dartmouth campus, the day has already heated up to 80 degrees and it's not quite eleven yet. A young man and woman, out to get their coffee drinks, eye me from half a block away. They look like undergrads sticking around college for the summer—for all I know, the same couple I passed climbing up Moosilauke two years back. The guy says, in a loud voice that seems meant more for me than for his girlfriend to hear, "It's going to get *hot* today." I round the corner, heading toward the edge of town.

The first section of the AT north out of Hanover looks rarely used—I find it overgrown with low bushes, still dripping wet from last night's rain. Soon my hiking shorts are soaked from wading through the groundcover. Finally the trail opens up near the first spring, and I stop to fold my bandana into a headband to keep the sweat out of my eyes. I move forward only a few steps when the air fills with clouds of insects—competing swarms of mosquitoes and blackflies—and I stop again to spray DEET on every exposed surface of my body. The poison slows down the mosquitoes but the blackflies persist, looking for holes in my defenses. They work their way under the edge of my headband, beneath the arms of my glasses near my ears, inside the neck of my T-shirt between my backpack straps. Their bites fester, turning into little hives that itch for days. I prefer the mosquitoes, but it's the blackflies winning the war over my blood.

With the heat—now up to 90 degrees—and the thick, humid air, the clouds of insects, the water dripping off the leaves and the mud squelching underfoot, my walk north through the Granite State feels more like a slog in the Amazonian rainforest. Even the mute creatures I encounter (no human being crosses my path) add to the jungle vibe: a spotted toad and two snakes: an inky dark Northern black racer and a yellow-striped garter snake two feet long. But the trees harbor red squirrels, not squirrel monkeys, and chickadees, not parrots, flit across the trail.

The short day, eleven miles from my car, ends at Moose Mountain shelter after a quick thousand foot climb up and over the mountain, where a stiff breeze keeps the bugs off at last and a view opens of purple thunderclouds streaming in from the west. A group of three section hikers, good natured guys in their forties, takes up one side of the roomy lean-to while two young women tent nearby. Half an hour later the storm hits in a big way, lightning striking the nearby summit and water pouring from the sky. The two young women sheepishly join us in the shelter, explaining that it's their first night on the Trail and they were told to tent rather than trust their luck sleeping next to strangers. We quickly put them at ease, teasing them just a little, and I move my sleeping bag to the center so that they can have one side to themselves.

With eighteen miles to hike and at least 3500 feet to climb I leave the shelter early, before the heat of day, but the cool aftermath of the storm lasts only a few short hours. The trail now drops again, losing almost a thousand feet, and once more I slog with wet boots through mud, overflowing streams, and clouds of biting insects. The climb up Smarts Mountain, 2300 feet above the trail's low point, at least takes me out of the muck and onto rock, but by now the temperature has risen back up to the high 80s. Then back down again to cross two swollen brooks, both of them bridged, before a final climb, another 700 feet, up Mount Cube as far as Hexacuba Shelter, where I flew off the icy privy steps and nearly knocked myself unconscious only a few months before. This time the rainstorm beats me to the shelter and I'm soaked to the bone before I've gained half the elevation. Then the rain stops as suddenly as it began and as I climb the last few hundred feet I'm puzzled to find the trail covered with small translucent globes the size of blueberries. I stop and peer at them: are they eggs laid by some migrating colony of salamanders or frogs? I pick one up and the cold pierces my fingertips. While rain was falling on me it was hailing higher up on the mountain. Soon the pellets of ice vanish as the air heats up again.

When I started hiking the AT I did not think I was hiking it by sections. Instead, I thought I was practicing for a thruhike, one I would begin in March of 2007, taking advantage of a planned sabbatical semester off. But with that date less than a year away, and nearly two years of "practice hikes" behind me, I'm starting to have serious second thoughts. Partly it has to do with the kids—how could they deal with my being away for five months, often unable even to call, so soon after the divorce? Partly it has to do with Dad, homebound, unable to drive anymore, in need of a part time aide to shop and clean and do laundry for him. I've already been managing Dad's finances from a distance and, my gut tells me, he will need much more help from me before long. And partly, to be honest, it's this damned heat, with the mud, and the bugs, and the sodden boots and clothes. If I leave Springer Mountain in mid-March as planned, I'll hit Vermont and southern New Hampshire just in time for peak blackfly season, for humid summer days and daily afternoon thunderstorms. Covering ground I've already mostly covered, hiking nearly five hundred miles all over again, including many long stretches of New England.

And I've come to love section hiking, despite the occasional trying day like this one. I love getting to know the Trail in different seasons. I've already put in at least a few days in every month from March to December, hiking through rhododendron tunnels in bloom, in light snows, in luminous October light, and, OK, in tropical summer heat. The tough little Boy Scout in me craves the challenge of a five-month two thousand miler, and my wild heart wants to live for months on end in the woods. But the hardy old guy I'm swiftly becoming likes a different challenge, the imperative to stay in hiking trim year after year, keeping up my strength, resisting entropy. And that same wild heart takes to the prospect of never losing sight of the mountains for more than a month or two at a time. Why not stretch it out, make hiking the Trail a decade long journey?

By the time I'm on my way the next morning, backtracking nine miles over Smarts Mountain to the Lyme-Dorchester Road, the decision has made itself. The sun quickly burns off the last wisps of morning fog and for the first time the humidity lifts as the mountains and I dry off together. Near the Smarts Mountain summit, hiking in full sun, I understand how, yes, I could do this for months—every one of the few items of clothing I carry can get soaking wet and, sooner or later, they will dry again. And I also understand that I don't have to do this for months. That, instead, I can keep section hiking throughout my fifties. I'm no longer in training for a future adventure. Without realizing it, I've been living the adventure for the past two years.

At the road crossing I make a stand a few yards off the trail and, for the first time in a quarter of a century, I put out my thumb. Twenty minutes later a pickup truck pulls over and I hop in; the young guy who has stopped for me will take me as far as Lyme, where I'll thumb a second ride back to Hanover. We've barely started moving when, just ahead of us, a small black bear lumbers across the road and into the brush on the other side. The driver and I both shout "Bear!" at the same time. As for the bear, it vanishes into a stand of hardwoods, heading east toward the Appalachian Trail.

July 2006. I'm racing along the smooth path that leads away from Kent Pond on a stretch of clipped, park-like grass when I encounter the first pig I have ever seen on a hike. Black colored and very round, it moves surprisingly fast, showing no fear and no interest in me, snuffling the earth. It is decidedly not a wild creature, though wild boars haunt the southern stretches of the AT. I know from the little bed symbol on the trail map that an inn or guesthouse lies close by so I assume this is someone's pet. I snap a picture of the pot-bellied pig for Lida and keep moving. I need to cover eighteen miles today and I want to bank as many miles as I can before it gets much hotter.

I left Boston early to reach the Long Trail Inn by ten, getting on the Trail near Maine Junction. From here the Long Trail, which shares a footpath with the AT south to the Massachusetts border, breaks away and heads north over the highest of the Green Mountains, stretching through Vermont's remote Northern Kingdom to dead end at the Canadian border. I promise myself to come back some year and finish the Long Trail, but today I stay with the AT as it hooks east. For the next forty-five miles the Trail stays comparatively low (barely climbing over 2600 feet) on its way toward the Connecticut River, where it crosses into New Hampshire and, soon after, reaches Hanover, where I began my last hike north. My section hikes don't always line up this neatly.

Given the elevation profile I feel good about the eighteen-mile day, even with a 10 a.m. start, but the heat worries me. Unlike last month's hike, this one promises several days of unbroken sun and, until they grow sweat sodden, I enjoy the sensation of dry wool socks inside dry boots. But the heat, as it climbs into the 80s, still grows oppressive even without the humidity. I think of Lida struggling up Sharon Mountain on another 80 degree July day, one year back, and I admit to myself how as I age I'm coming to share her allergy to backpacking in the heat. Today, though, I feel bound to keep up my two miles an hour, determined to reach camp by 7 though it will stay light till 8:30.

In addition to the domestic pig I see chipmunks, a warty American toad, and various thrushes pecking near the trail. Spring beauties are out today in force; otherwise, I notice few wildflowers. The modest ups and downs accumulate, adding to at least 3000 feet of gain in all, as the trail climbs over Quimby Mountain, a sawtooth collection of unnamed hills, and a final steep stretch up Sawyer Hill. On this last climb, just a few hundred feet up, I suddenly feel nauseous and light-headed. I sit down and drink the last pint of my water, which I've been hoarding, and realize I have let myself get dehydrated. Luckily I soon find the stream at Winturri Shelter running high and clear—so clear I don't bother treating the water despite the low elevation. As always, I experience no ill effects, though I've gone against one of my own rules of thumb (always treat water sources located under 2500 feet, as well as water from active beaver ponds, from muddy springs, from any stream that might flow down past a livestock pasture—or Boy Scout encampment—and from established sites that look trashed or otherwise skanky).

Although it's peak hiking season I have the shelter to myself—just as well because I feel too tired to set up my tent. In the dusk a ground bird comes scratching right in front of the shelter edge: the size of a meadowlark, though plumper, and with a meadowlark's black neck ring, though it has a dun-colored, streaked breast. It can only be a bobwhite, drawn north, I suppose, by the summer heat. Later, in my unzipped sleeping bag, I hear the soft striking of hooves on the ground as a group of deer passes through in the dark.

I take the next day easy, sleeping in a bit with just twelve miles to cover. In between short climbs and descents, the trail meanders through third growth forests marked with ancient stone fences, traverses fallow fields, and crosses a number of small streams, a pleasant walk in the country despite the heat that once more comes on strong and early. The bobwhite quail turns out to be only the first in a series of game birds that haunt this stretch of Vermont. First a woodcock flies across the trail just a few feet away, then I scare up at least a dozen grouse hiking across Thistle Hill: they startle and burst into flight one by one, as if waiting for their turns. Though a wind picks up in the evening and promises a change in the weather, I tent near the shelter to take advantage of the built-in bug screening and sleep on top of my bag—it's so hot I have to force myself to eat. I wake at 5:15 to get started ahead of the rain and watch a fox circling the campsite and making its bird-like territorial barks as I cook an early breakfast. Just as I get back from the shelter stream the skies open and I head out in a downpour.

The rain makes for a welcome change, cooling the air and giving me back my stamina. When it tapers off five or six red efts crawl out to slither in the mud and, during a lunch break at Happy Hill shelter, a wood thrush nonchalantly forages in the duff a few feet in front of me. (I've been hearing thrush songs each dawn and each evening). Once the trail reaches Norwich it's mostly quick, dull road walking through town, across I-91 and the Connecticut River, and into Hanover, where I reach the Hanover Inn at 1:50, ten minutes early. Wet, dirty, and bedraggled, I'm almost embarrassed to ask even for an outdoor table. But the smiling young hostess—another Dartmouth student?—could not be more gracious. Soon Joel turns up and we order beers and sandwiches. Joel is the only one of my good friends who has been divorced himself, so I quickly find myself opening up, relieved that I can tell him about the coming breakup without being judged. Lunch over, we somehow manage to squeeze my backpack into the trunk of his dark green Miata. We drive to the Long Trail Inn with the top down and settle in for a long evening of drinking and talk: we have no secrets from one another. And I realize that there's one more good reason to keep section hiking: it gives me an excuse to get together with old friends.

July 2009. The Presidential traverse through the heart of the White Mountains, like the Smokies, the Virginia Highlands, and the balds of North Carolina, makes for one of the literal highpoints of the Appalachian Trail. The trail climbs steeply out of Crawford Notch, up the Webster Cliffs, and over Mounts Webster and Jackson before descending a bit to Mizpah Spring. Then it climbs back over the 4000 foot mark and stays above timberline for at least a dozen rugged miles, either summiting or just skirting the tops of Mounts Pierce (4312'), Eisenhower (4760'), and Monroe (5372'), the southern Presidentials. You climb even more to the summit of Mount Washington, at 6288 feet the highest point in the Northeast and the highest point on the AT north of the Tennessee line. Then just a modest descent to follow the Gulfside ridge over the northern Presidentials: Jefferson (5716'), Adams (5799'), and Madison (5366'). Soon after summiting Madison the trail plunges down a chaos of boulders lining the Madison Gulf and the Great Gulf, a long, punishing descent. At last the trail levels off a few miles north of Pinkham Notch, crossing over a suspension bridge into a stream-laced forest where I will walk straight into a moose.

The November before I had taken a weekend out and back to hike the AT from the Webster Cliffs to the Naumann Tentsite. So today I can take the shorter, easier route to Mizpah Spring on the old Crawford Path, a horse trail dating back to the early 1800s. The Crawford Path merges with the AT near Mizpah Spring, where I stop for water before heading further north. Morning mists come and go, cooling the long, high ridge walk to the summit of Pierce. I had worried about another hot summer hike but the temperature stays below the mid 60s; the breezes whipping at the exposed rock make for almost chilly walking in shorts and T-shirt. Once over Mount Pierce, the path alternates between rocky climbs and gentler ascents over subalpine meadows, where bare rock yields in places to heath-like vegetation, not so much low growing as horizontal, dotted with tiny flowerets: Mountain Avens, Diapensia, Mountain Cranberry, and Labrador Tea. The high meadows then give way to austere stretches of felsenmeer, rock-strewn lakes of coarse-grained schist, formed by endless freeze and thaw cycles that shatter the high rock slabs and leave behind a litter of broken stone. In the soft late morning light the landscape looks almost unearthly, Martian or lunar, yet here one walks over the very bones of the earth, stripped bare of soil and vegetation.

Clouds keep lowering and then lifting again, when the band of clear blue between grey rock and pearl grey sky opens to reveal hundreds of peaks to the south and east. Memories also also come and go with this or that turn in the path. I think back to the cold, dark, drizzly night eight months ago, shivering in the Naumann tentsite, one of the rare times I felt lonely in the mountains. And then I recall my walk with Nate over this very trail four years ago during a two-night family trip to the Mizpah hut in honor of my fiftieth birthday. Nate hiked so strongly that day and, for a change, without a single complaint, indulging me, I suppose, on account of my birthday. We left the hut early to cover twelve tough miles from Mizpah Spring Hut to the top of Washington and back, returning a good hour before dinner. And I cringe when I remember, too, how I had stipulated that Lida and her mom would stay behind to do their own shorter hike, knowing that otherwise we would never summit Washington in time to get back to the hut before dark. That led to a lot of bad feelings, as I suppose I should have known. We never backpacked as a family again.

For a bleak moment I'm certain that this had meant the end: the turning point, the single bad call when for selfish reasons, a birthday hike I just had to do, I squandered my children's birthright of an intact family. Yet soon enough I realize how very many passages over twenty contentious years I could pick out as *the* fatal moment, if I really thought that life worked that way, that marriages lived or died by any single event short of outright tragedy. Still, as I walk flashes of pleasure and guilt, sheer happiness and bitter remorse keep coming and going like the mist and the clouds, like the rise and fall of the trail.

Since I'm not in a hurry I walk easily, gaining over 3,000 feet in elevation with little conscious effort. I even forget to stop and rest after my one break for water at Mizpah, so I reach my day's goal, Lakes of the Clouds Hut, not long after 2 p.m. The twin lakes—little tarns, really—look pristine and inviting: despite the cloudy weather, I'd be tempted to swim if they did not seem as delicate as the alpine vegetation around them. Instead I take a walk on the mysterious Dry River Trail, remote and untraveled looking, and notice a sign promising a shelter a few more miles into the Dry River wilderness. Another trip to make some day to come.

By the time I get back the hut has started filling up, pairs of hiking buddies, a large group of teens, and a scattering of families, including a couple of ringers for the happy backpacking family I once hoped would be my own. In the packed dining hall I feel lonely again, the odd single, and I wonder if I should have made a longer day and camped at that Dry River Wilderness shelter. I leave early the next morning to get ahead of the crowd, enjoying the morning cool and reaching Mount Washington before ten. The approach to Washington over the AT in summer makes for a bizarre enough experience. After miles of treading carefully through pristine alpine zones, as rare as they are fragile, staying rigorously, even reverently, on the beaten path, the final ascent of Washington brings hordes of tourists into view. Their cars strain up the Auto Road and, making things still worse, this morning the Cog Railway train belches thick clouds of coal black smoke as it chugs still more tourists to the summit. It comes as a shock and, to me, it feels like a desecration of one of the high places long held sacred, by the Abenaki and by the early mountaineers alike. Climbers who have spent much time here in the winter, when the peak becomes forbidding again, claim that spirits still haunt the mountaintop. Some report feeling the presence of a guardian spirit, but most speak in darker tones of some obscure wrathful force pushing them towards danger.

If the sprits are angry ones, I can't say I blame them, given what the summit has become. Yet I also remember how happy Nate was, four years earlier, when I indulged him in a double cheeseburger and fries as I ate my roll, cheese, and apple in the Visitor Center cafeteria, the first and last time I ever visited it. I expect many a thruhiker has been even happier to get a calorie splurge in so unlikely a place. Still, I would love to see the road closed and the cog railway shut down, carrying the disassembled parts of the visitor center on its last trip down the mountain.

I rush to get water before the gaggle of tourists thickens and hasten toward the rough, rocky path to the east. The skies clear in time for long views in every direction, reminding me again of the brilliantly clear October day Nate and I hiked Mount Washington four years ago. The trail edges around the summit of Mount Clay and then makes a rocky descent to the shallow col before climbing again high on the shoulder of Mount Jefferson, where I take the short summit trail to the top. Then it leads down again to a deeper col, a high mountain oasis with a strong flowing spring, trickling streams, and lush groundcover. The stand of dwarf evergreens here are only trees for miles in either direction. I just stop briefly before hiking on to Thunderstorm Junction and then up the summit trail to the top of Mount Adams. I have lunch on the mountaintop, with a full view of Washington and a hundred lesser peaks clustered all around. Two days in the high places have left me with eyes that feel bigger, a gaze that feels keener.

I reach Madison Springs hut by mid-afternoon with plenty of time to rest my feet. The thick callouses still remaining from last May's long hike through New Jersey and New York have started hurting, rubbed and squeezed by miles of schist and granite. For the second time in two days the sunset lures me out of the hut for a long sit on a flat rock away from the noise. Yesterday the sun dropped dramatically, a globe of orange fire descending out of a high band of clouds only to quickly disappear again beneath the horizon. Today the sunset is more horizontal ooze than vertical drop, slowly spreading a red-orange glow over the western peaks and ridges, rich and mellow and subtle.

I make my own early breakfast the next day, alone in the dining area, fighting my gag reflex to suck down a double shot of cold liquid condensed coffee (a one-time experiment). By 6:45 I'm moving fast on the trail up Madison, looming some 500 feet above the hut. I linger only a few moments on the summit before heading down even faster. I'm trying to get back to Boston in time for a samba class, of all things, but the trail, even rockier than yesterday, threatens to slow me down despite the rapid elevation loss. Once down the summit path the trail stretches for awhile into long, loping ridges that bring me back to the North Cascades, but soon after it begins plunging down and over a seemingly endless series of boulders, outcroppings, and tricky slabs of schist just coarse enough to give a little purchase to worn bootsoles. Stopping only once for a long drink of water I continue to test my legs. Going down a steep trail is notoriously harder on aging legs than going up, but my knees, after nearly fifty four years of use, stand up nicely against the shocks of short leaps and controlled slides. I try to stay high, rock hopping in the northwestern style of hiking, and after a few hours I at last arrive at the first stands of krumholz, still interspersed with stretches of sheer rock.

Always losing altitude, but more gradually, the trail at last begins to amble through shady woods, crossed by more and more streams and rills and growing mossy and lush, a delicious contrast to the austere rocky world above. At one turn I'm startled to see the chestnut flanks of a large horse on the trail. No!—it's a moose, a cow, standing directly ahead of me on the path. Huge and splendid, she stands her ground, though every so often a ripple along her haunch shows how tense she must feel, confronted by so strange an animal as myself. As she keeps still for several long minutes, blocking my way, I try to relax my own tension, breathing from my belly, enjoying this rare chance to stand as close to a moose as I would ever want. Hoping, too, that she doesn't come any closer or linger with me *too* much longer.

Finally a noise in the forest, a snapped stick or branch, causes her to leap into the brush and disappear into thick tree cover. Happy and also running late, I jog down the old Jackson Road trail to the AMC lodge at Pinkham Notch, where I left my car and caught a shuttle three days earlier. After a look behind at Mount Washington I speed toward Boston, where I somehow arrive in time for a quick shower. Soon I'm in a Cambridge dance studio practicing samba steps on sore legs and lightly blistered feet. Back home a few hours later I fall asleep still excited, still seeing the moose.

August-September 2009. The Austin Brook Trail, off North Road, will take me directly to Gentian Pond, where I turned around on my first hike in the Mahoosucs the year before. So I give something extra to Bruce, the shuttle guy, grateful he could even find the obscure trailhead, before climbing some 1300 feet straight into the heart of this wild, rugged mountain range. The late summer day starts sunny and cool, temperatures in the 50s, my favorite hiking weather. And I feel a surge of happiness, with two full days to spend on what has already become one of my favorite stretches of the AT.

When I reach the first, bare summit, Mount Success, after climbing another 1400 feet, the winds blow cold. On the ridge they gust at speeds of up to 60 miles an hour, winds to face down and wrestle through. And then, descending into a sun-warmed col, all grows peaceful again, quiet and remote. Up or down, the terrain stays rough—I use both hands climbing up wet rock and have to risk short slides back down toward the sections of flatter terrain. The flat stretches go through subalpine meadow alternating with patches of bog and classic Northern woods, spruce and pine and paper birch. The trail crosses from New Hampshire into Maine, though state borders seem meaningless up here, and again climbs sharply, another 600 feet up Mount Carlo, where it stays high on ridges and rocky knobs and carpets of red moss.

Just when the elevation gain—maybe 3000 feet in all today—and the scrappy terrain is starting to get to me, I take a step forward on a rotting bog bridge and my foot goes right through until I find myself literally bogged down, my right leg sunk up to the crotch in soft, oozy peat. Luckily the plank beside the rotten one holds, so I stay crouched on one leg and exert all my strength to pull out the other one, a stubborn cork in a tight bottleneck. It takes maybe five minutes of patient, relentless pulling. Just as the leg starts to pop out a whole crew of hikers appears over the ridgeline to the north: "Need any help?" And the wonderful absurdity of it all hits me as my leg lifts free: the ground that disappears from under me, the striding backpacker transformed into a pathetic, one-legged creature, the sudden audience that shows up in the middle of the wilderness on a day I've seen no one till that moment. "Thanks, I'm OK now." And I am.

The hardy band of hikers turns out to be a mountain rescue group; freed from the muck, I can see them half guiding, half carrying a backpacker whose shoulder has been yanked out of its socket by a slip on the rocks. So I walk on feeling grateful that my own mishap has left me with nothing worse than a wet pants leg and a good story. Aside from the bog bridges and the occasional splotch of white paint, the trail shows virtually no signs of human contrivance. It follows long ribbons of granite along the ridgelines and traces dry streambeds lower down, meanders over bare, weathered summits and angles sharply down over rock slides, only to lead to yet another scramble up a rough, stony face. It takes everything I have to keep moving at a decent pace, so I'm both surprised and impressed when I pass a plucky old guy—"old" meaning, now that I'm pushing 54, at least 65. He gives me a message for his friend up the trail and I quickly leave him behind.

When I come upon the friend, who looks closer to 70, I've just eased myself down a nearly vertical slab, with a narrow landing space before the even steeper one just ahead. I find him resting, leaning back at a 70 degree angle against the rocks behind him; when I come to a stop the narrow rock landing leaves only a foot or so of distance between us. I tell him his friend is on his way and he locks eyes with me, looking at me in a way I can only describe as beseechingly. For a moment I think he means to ask me to help him down to the next shelter, another mile and a half away, something I don't much want to do. He reaches his right hand out toward me, his hiking poles in his other hand. "Sometimes," he says, smiling more at himself than at me, "you just need a little pull." And then I realize he might as well be a beetle on its back, powerless as he is to lift his own weight and that of his backpack up to standing. I take his hand in mine—his knuckles are crusted with recently dried blood—and yank him up. Then I look for a reasonable way down and end up half sliding, half leaping to the next good foothold, where I land with a hard jolt. The old guy looks on sadly—neither of us knows how he will manage this latest vertical drop.

I reach the Full Goose lean-to at 6:30 and grab one of the last spaces inside with every available tentsite already taken. Two more old guys—these ones quite spry looking—are waiting for their two friends and, miraculously, the last two spots in the shelter stay unclaimed until they roll in shortly after sunset, looking relieved and exhausted. Lights out in the shelter comes early tonight. No one mentions the next day's terrain, though I expect everyone is thinking about it. The shelter stands only a mile and a half south of the Mahoosuc Notch, what decades of hikers have called the hardest single mile of the AT.

I start through it by 8:30 the next morning, ahead of the crowd. The Notch is a long, gently declining gorge choked with boulders, some car-sized, some house-sized, jumbled and jostled together every which way like a maze set up by a puckish mountain god. I take a long minute to check the conditions—the rock surface has mostly dried by now and its rough texture promises to keep skidding to a minimum. I remember the advice of a repeat thruhiker I met in a campsite somewhere in North Carolina: "Stay high as much as you can." Crawling between and under the boulders can take up to four hours. I'm determined to go faster than that.

So I reach back to all the rockslides and boulder fields of my Washington State youth and leap. Knowing it may be the last time I can hike this way (those bloodied knuckles), I start what I call "cascading," leaping from one boulder to the next, trying to use momentum and gravity to keep airborne, thinking with my feet, trusting to my body. Gary Snyder calls this a kind of "irregular dancing" in a passage of *Practice of the Wild* that I once read with a flash of recognition: a dance of jumps and sidesteps, the eye "looking ahead, picking the foothold to come, while never missing the step of the moment." Body, mind, rock converge in a wild, unpredictable rhythm. "The mountain," he writes, channeling Dōgen, "keeps up with the mountain."

I step, leap, twist in the air and sometimes come to a dead stop when the gap ahead yawns impossibly wide or the next rock presents a sheer wall. Then I squeeze, crawl, slither—whatever works to keep moving until I can clamber back up to the light. The temperature drops a good twenty degrees in the shade of the ravine; at every step water drips, gurgles, and echoes from an unseen streambed somewhere below. Three times I have to take off my backpack and push it ahead or pull it behind me. The rocks scrape against skin and boot leather, send jarring shocks of impact through my knees and up my spine, but they never betray me: every foothold sticks.

I get through the Notch in just over ninety minutes, feeling exhilarated and a little used up. Then the trail angles up dramatically, climbing more than a thousand feet to the top of the Mahoosuc Arm in just over a mile. All the time I gained dancing through the Notch I lose dragging my body up this pitiless rock face. My dreamlike return to adolescence ends with the first few hundred feet of elevation and it's a tired, fifty-three year old man who at last tops out on a smooth granite knob.

A mile beyond and the landscape transforms yet again, this time into a lushly wooded basin, only a few hundred feet below the summit of the Arm yet a complete change from the subalpine terrain of the past two days. More lake than tarn, pretty Speck Pond looks clear, calm, and inviting—a few degrees warmer and a quick swim would be hard to resist. Instead I follow the trail up toward Speck Mountain and then sharply down, over two thousand feet of elevation loss in just two miles, toward Grafton Notch. The steep descent proves just as rugged as most of the climbs and does little to speed things up—I reach the Notch and my waiting car at 4:30, nine hours to cover ten miles. I feel a cold coming on and I know how badly my legs will ache the next day; I miss the turn onto NH115 and go thirty miles out of the way. And it's all good. I don't know how it could be much better.

August 2013. The clouds darken from purple to nearly black ten miles out of Monson and within minutes we're driving into a wall of rain. I think the rain can't get any heavier and it does; I think it has to start tailing off any moment now and it doesn't. So I ask Gerry, a Maine furniture maker turned shuttle driver, to pull over at the next gas station we come to with an overhang. If I try to get on my rain gear in a deluge like this I'll be soaked through before I can get my parka out of the top of my backpack.

Then, within a mile or two of Grafton Notch, the downpour turns into a sprinkle and at last stops altogether. Gerry parks in the middle of the lot, away from the dripping trees. I take off my rain jacket but leave the garbage bag kilt and packcover on for now, since the skies look almost as dark as before. Then I walk to the roadway and look for the gap in the bushes that will mark the trail going north. There isn't a sign or so much as a single white blaze in sight. I go back through the parking area to see where the AT comes in from the south, with no clear memory of just where I got out of the woods four years ago.

I spot the trailhead just as a hiker emerges from it. He looks to be in his late 50s, he's almost exactly my height and build, and even his hair has turned the same shade of ash gray as mine. He points up to the New England Patriot's cap on his head as he tells me his trailname. Patriot has about 270 miles to go in order to complete his thruhike and looks more than good for it; I can't help thinking of him as the thruhiker I decided not to become.

Together we cross the road and find the trailhead north, hike together for a bit, and then start leapfrogging one another. The rain mostly holds off and almost immediately I find myself immersed in the rugged, untamed Maine woods that I love. Only—they turn out to be more rugged even than I expected. Somehow, somewhere I had picked up the notion that north of the Mahoosucs the Trail gets easier. While there's nothing quite like the Notch or the Arm just to the south, this stretch of AT proves almost as tough. Tiring ups (with 2400 feet to gain over the first four miles) and steep downs, tall rock faces to scale or slipslide down, rocky descents that call for giant steps or short leaps, a choice between straining the thighs or punishing the knees. I had planned to cover at least fourteen miles a day, rather than the ten to twelve mile days I had averaged in the Mahoosucs. What was I thinking?

The rain starts falling hard again three miles from the day's destination, a spring just north of Surplus Pond, then tapers off in time for me to set up my tent and cook a quick dinner. The campsite only has space for two or three tents and, as a young thruhiker has already claimed the higher ground, I choose a spot lower down rather than crowding him. Which I begin to regret early in the morning as the rain, coming down harder than ever, forms a puddle that floats the top third of my tent floor. Somehow, the ultrathin fabric and the bathtub design keep the water out and my sleeping bag dry, but the tent seems to have gained a pound of water weight when I pack up quickly during a brief letup in the downpour.

The short hike up Wyman Mountain should be easy but today the rain has turned the trail, ordinarily a dry creek bed, into a rushing stream. I take awkward, bowlegged strides trying to avoid the deep channel in the middle, but the sides of the path become so muddy that my boots fill with water anyway.

After about a mile I experience one of those trail illusions I thought had stopped occurring a year or two earlier: a high female voice singing in some unknown language from far up the trail. But it is no illusion. Soon two or three other voices join and, a minute or two later, the lead singer appears over a short rise, a high school age French Canadian girl, fine featured, soaked through, singing in Quebecois. As her friends catch up she asks me if there's a pond coming up soon: it seems that now that they are thoroughly wet they want to make it official with a good plunge. I tell her if there wasn't one before there's definitely one by now and they move on, followed by at least half a dozen others.

I like their attitude but I can't bring myself to share it: I simply do not want to get this wet this early in the hike, especially given the threat of blisters. The trail is all mud, slick rock, bog, and running water and I tire quickly, with three mountains still to climb before I reach the day's goal. Then I come to the first ford.

Maine fords (which largely take the place of bridges further south) are completely unpredictable: what someone found an easy rock hop a few days earlier can be a thigh deep slog through rushing water after forty hours of heavy rain. This ford comes up to my crotch—without my faithful stick I would not be able to stay on my feet. The climb up Moody Mountain is like Wyman, only much steeper, and at the ford on the other side the water rises to my waist. Fighting the current leaves me only more exhausted and frustrated than before.

Then at the other side I spot Patriot lacing up his boots. We hike the first mile or so up Old Blue together, chatting off and on, and as long as I'm with my new friend I forget my bad mood and my worries about the day ahead and just hike. Then the trail turns to near vertical rock and Patriot takes off, saying "I gotta turn on the jets." I tell him I must have left my jets at home and watch him vanish from sight more quickly than I would have thought possible.

The rain keeps coming and the day grows interminable. Finally I begin the fourth ascent, up Bemis Mountain, on the other side of which the lean-to I am aiming for should finally come into view. But the ascent seems to go on forever, a series of tough climbs up false summits that make me feel I'm stuck in some backpacker's nightmare. I had set out to hike seventeen miles and at the pace I've been reduced to I simply won't finish before dark. I can only hope the trail gets more reasonable once I am over the summit, assuming I can drag myself up and over the steep rocks that lead to it. Steep and slippery—twice my stick saves me from a hard fall and then, as I desperately jab down with it once more, it catches in the rift between two blocks of granite and I hear a crack. I quickly pull the stick back out and look it over—I can't see even a thin line on it so it must have cracked deep inside. I have no idea whether it will hold up or snap clean the next time I put my full weight on it. And I actually plead with it out loud, my hiking stick of eight hundred miles: "Just get me to the top, buddy. Please."

Dark is gathering as I crest the peak—it's nearly eight p.m.—and I look around in vain for someplace to camp. The woods beneath the ridge loom up steep, dense, and nearly impenetrable, a century or two of fallen trees and branches filling every available space. I would have to sleep sitting up. I reach the north end of the summit and the trail angles down just as steeply as it came up, a chaos of dark, wet rock that looks hard enough to negotiate in full daylight. Hiking down it in the dark, with only the pale beam of my ultralight headlamp to guide me, could easily result in a broken arm or leg—or neck.

Desperately backtracking in the waning light I scan both sides of the trail again and, this time, I just make out a faint deer trail leading toward the dropoff on the other side of the ridge. It leads through rocks and bushes to a narrow overlook where the ground flattens just enough for me to lay out my tiny backpacking tent; there is even a patch of earth I can drive most of the stakes into. Even so, one tent wall pushes against some low bushes and the opening rests on a slab of flat rock that ends just a few yards away in a sheer drop. Not a good night for sleepwalking.

The rain has tailed off and summit breezes cool the air without chilling it. Well out of sight of the trail, perched on the edge of a wild world, I feel solitary and relieved and strangely happy. And deeply grateful for what to me is the ultimate example of "trail magic": chance has led me to the one bare, horizontal patch on the mountain I can just squeeze a tent into on the one night I need it the most. Darkness and silence set in all around me. I sleep a delicious sleep on the top of Bemis Mountain.

In the morning light I see that the bushes pushing against my tent are dotted with tiny, ripe blueberries and I gather a handful to mix in with my oatmeal, cooked on the narrow span of flat rock in front of my tent. The rain has ended but the two days of heavy downpours have left the rock almost slimy. I slip and fall twice during the steep descent—I never would have made it down in one piece the night before. I gain back the two miles I missed by hiking from soon after dawn to near dusk, a long thirteen-hour day, and over the next few days I hike from early light to sunset without fail. Each evening I arrive almost too tired to cook and, for the first time ever, too tired to write in my trail journal, let alone read. The fords become thigh deep, then knee deep, and finally I feel ready to break out my dry socks. It turns out that I have packed the wrong pair—a larger size I bought by accident and somehow got mixed in with my hiking clothes—and I develop strange new blisters on the bottoms of both feet. The occasional road crossings now feature "Missing" signs for Geraldine Largay, a woman in her mid-sixties who mysteriously disappeared, two weeks earlier, while hiking this same section of the AT. (Her body will be found two years later in dense woods less than a mile off the trail; according to her journal she was still alive, slowly starving to death in a makeshift tentsite, as I climbed out of Grafton Notch.) Six days into a planned eleven-day hike a voice in my head that is both mine and my son's says, almost audibly, "Dad, you should *definitely* bail."

Not that I'm having no fun at all on this trip. After all, I'm hiking through one of my favorite places in the world. Especially once the sun comes out after three sodden days, I can appreciate the sheer wildness opening up on all sides in this region of rotting blowdowns, bogs, rock, unbridged streams, and glacial ponds, over trails that often become no more than occasional paint marks on rock slides, steep granite slabs, and (for now) dry streambeds. Juncos and white throated sparrows flit by, I flush a pair of grouse who fly off in opposite directions, one calling noisily to distract me from the other, wild blueberries ripen on the sunny ridges, and the ancient forests below offer shady cool. Winds blow through the campsite at night, toads squat on the trail and a dozen varieties of toadstool grow beside it, diapensia blooms on the summits. The notches and stream valleys, warmed by the August sun, fill with the sweet smell of balsam fir and the darker, resiny scent of spruce trees.

One night, at the end of a fourteen mile, eleven hour day, I find a half hidden tentsite off the trail in the glacial cirque hemmed in by South and North Crocker Mountains. I camp on a little knoll overlooking a swamp in a space not too much bigger than the one I just squeezed into on top of Bemis. A perfect spot to spy out a moose in the dusk or in early light. No moose arrives, but darkness comes in and the woods grow perfectly quiet, a calm so deep it feels strangely exciting, a solitude so perfect it extinguishes any hint of loneliness. The utter wildness all around me rekindles the wildness within. I remember why I am here.

Tomorrow would be a good day to bail.

I hike into Stratton the next morning on feet that feel like they've been soundly bastinadoed (a lovely word Brian and I picked up as boys from the pirate books Dad used to read us). I make it to town just ahead of a fresh spell of rain and arrange a shuttle for the next morning back to Shaw's Boarding House in Monson. I don't need to explain my early arrival when I get to Shaw's—they've heard it all before. I tell them to look for me next August. And then I'm on my way home, already planning next year's hike as I drive.

August 2014. At some point I read in a Trail magazine that completion rates for thruhikes do not show any correlation with the age of the hiker. Until, that is, the hiker turns 60, when completed hikes grow less likely with every additional year of age. So I decide to finish hiking the AT before I'm out of my 50s. I have a little over a year left for that to happen.

The failed attempt to hike over 150 miles of rugged Maine trail in ten and a half days has forced me to acknowledge my own aging. I simply cannot count on my body to stay as resilient as it was a decade earlier, even with exercise routines and frequent weekend hikes. So this time, heading back to Monson and a shuttle south to Stratton, I give myself a generous full week to cover the 75 miles I left unwalked the year before. I plan to take my time, to enjoy a short day or two, and to stop and rest more often during the day.

I'm also wearing my first internal frame backpack—an Osprey, like Patriot's—and find immediately that it really does redistribute the packload in a way that magically cancels out a good ten pounds. It also does away with the potentially dangerous sway effect that can make you teeter on high rocks and knife-edge ridges, pulling you toward a nasty fall. I leave my external frame backpack, not much different from the one I bought at the original REI in Seattle forty years earlier, in the back of my gear closet. The Mr. Old School act has worn thin.

I'm still sporting my wooden hiking stick, though, wrapped tightly with five layers of duct tape where it started to crack on Bemis Mountain. The tape only adds to its charm. I figure it's good for another 600 miles, which is close to the length of Appalachian Trail I have yet to cover.

Today, though, I only have to hike ten and a half miles—while gaining at least 3500 feet on the steep upward trek from the Stratton Brook valley to the top of two-horned Bigelow Mountain. A beautiful summer day, hot at first but cooling down as the trail passes above 3,000, then 4,000 feet. And a great day for admiring the local fungi, toadstools and mushrooms and tree ears and clusters of vertical shoots in banana yellow and mango orange like spiky alien hair, probably two species of coral fungus. Red cap mushrooms on white stalks (fly agarics) like the ones in the Peter Rabbit books, brown and beige ones like in the grocery store (honey mushrooms and king boletes), and some all bright red and all coal black mushrooms which I cannot identify. Plus the fungus-like flower Indian Pipe, as well as diapensia and a nameless four-leaved plant with red berries. I stop at lovely, secretive Horns Pond, tucked between the south and north horns of Bigelow, for a long lunch before summiting, with Flagstaff Lake spread out gigantically below. The day ends at woodsy Safford Notch campsite after a two thousand foot descent, where I find a tentsite close enough to the stream that I can fall asleep listening to the ageless music of water on stone. Two wood thrushes help me wake up around 5:30 the next morning, competing over which can sing the most hauntingly beautiful song.

By the time I've reached the broad summit of Little Bigelow the winds come up, blowing thin ribbons of cirrus clouds across the bright summer sky, threatening a change in the weather. (Trail talk has it that a big rain is one day off.) The flat summit stretches out over two miles, beautiful hiking on soft earth with lots of duff to cushion it, chickadees flitting all around, more fungi lining the path, one old birch tree covered with odd bell-shaped growths, horse hoof fungi. Then down to walk a muddy, scenic mile along the edge of Flagstaff Lake, a short climb or two, and an early arrival at West Carry Pond (named for an ancient portage system) in time for a long swim. Lazing by the water, letting the air dry me, I hear a kingfisher squawking but fail to spot it. At night loons call across the pond and a coyote howls back from the woods.

Racing against the portended rainstorm I head out by 6:30, just ten reasonably horizontal miles to cover over rocks and roots, bog bridges and lovely stretches of woodland trail covered with brown pine needles and last fall's decaying leaves. All day clouds fill the sky, light to dark grey, making for quick, cool hiking, even quicker over the new bog bridges along East Carry Pond, the next open water link along the old canoe trail. The clouds obligingly hold back and I reach my destination, Pierce Pond, in time to lay out my gear in the shelter just as the first good sprinkle begins. I'm determined to swim again so I leave the shelter nude, wanting to keep my clothes dry, and wade into the water, warmish near the rocky edge, cool but not chilly where it goes deeper. Somehow

I manage to dry out in a very light rain, pierced by scattered gleams of sunlight, water bugs leaving tiny circular wakes on the pond surface that contrast with the ripple patterns the wind makes.

I spend the long afternoon exploring, visiting Harrison's Camp at the other end of the pond and taking in the view from the rocks just below the shelter. Gray clouds above, gray shore below, granite rocks lining the banks, dark blue-green hills in the further distance, a round wooded hill looming over the pond, various points and peninsulas pushing into the water and covered, like the near hill, in evergreen hues. By late afternoon an exuberant, hardy group of young thruhikers begins to arrive. The first of them, a round-faced, sweet-natured blonde named Acorn, wades into the pond in a steady thin rain and swims across, back, across, back for a good hour despite having hiked eighteen miles that day. When her friends arrive she organizes a walk to Harrison's Camp, though by now the skies have really opened up, claiming that she has "too much energy." They all join her after setting up their tents, expertly and uncomplainingly, in the pouring rain.

The next morning we all start out for a short day to the Northern Outdoors Center, where some will pick up maildrops and do laundry and all will drink beers, eat burgers, and sleep in soft beds. First, though, we have to get across the Kennebec River. Too broad, swift, and unpredictable to ford without courting a watery death, the Kennebec stands out as the only section of the AT done not by foot but by boat. I get to the crossing early, wanting to hike alone ahead of the gang, and settle in to a meditative half hour on the riverbank, listening to the current and watching the mist drift over the water. Right on schedule the ferryman shoots me a gap-toothed smile from across the river and eases a red canoe over the rocks. By now the first knot of young thruhikers has caught up to me and one of them, Shivers, agrees to share the first ride. I grab a paddle and take the bow end while Shivers sits in the middle like a frontier princess, waving to her friends and smiling like a happy little kid. At the other side she sits on a rock, waiting for the rest of her bunch, while I head down the road for eighteen hours of civilized living.

The fifteen miles from the north bank of the Kennebec to Bald Mountain Brook turns out to be one of the most beautiful days yet. Blue skies alternate with a light grey cloud cover, rain threatens at times but always holds off. From the Kennebec to Pleasant Pond the trail cuts through a hardwood forest over soft earth, with bright green moss and more fungi in tropical colors lining the path. I stop to watch the loons before climbing the thousand feet straight up Pleasant Pond Mountain, moving quickly, feeling strong and energetic after two short days. The light constantly changes as the skies brighten and dim and brighten again, colors glow vividly after the recent rain, and at the higher elevations I feel at times like I am back in the North Cascades: rocks, rills, bog bridges, lush evergreen woods, rugged climbs and flatter stretches over ridges and along rushing streams. Then down again, with a few ups, to still another glacial pond, Moxie, a ribbon of blue-grey cutting through dark green woods viewed from above, a chilly ford, crotch high, where the trail cuts across its south end.

Then *more* pretty hiking, everything glowing, dazzling, water, duff, leaves, rocks, white blazes, glistening roots—amazing. The rain continues to hold off as I climb up to Bald Mountain Brook lean-to, where I meet some friendly southbounders my age, Coffee John and Valley Blue, who are doing the mirror version of my own hike, Monson to Stratton. I feel grateful for the company after dark, when sounds that could be either firecrackers or gunshots echo within hearing. (I would much rather have a bear visit the shelter than a group of rowdy locals.) But nothing happens amiss: just another night in the Maine woods.

Next morning I follow long ribbons of granite up to the summit of Moxie Bald where wide vistas open up in every direction, including the long, slender shape of Moxie Pond gleaming to the south. Coming down I scare up a female ruffed grouse who merely flits up to perch on a nearby tree, making clucking noises to draw my attention. Somewhere near me in the bushes tiny *peeps* answer her call. Now the trail gets damp, then muddy, then boggy, and another easy day, thirteen miles, turns into a wet slog. Temporary brooks stream across the path, some nearly impossible to get around, and the first ford, a thigh deep crossing over submerged logs, tells how much harder and longer it must have rained on this side of the mountain. The next two fords prove still deeper, the water lapping up toward my waist, and the last one, where the trail cuts across a fork of the Piscataquis, features a hard, fast current, but someone has kindly stretched a cord across the water that helps me keep my balance.

Then the footpath at last grows drier, covered now with brown pine needles, as it follows the main branch of the Piscataquis east toward Monson. At last, after nearly eight hours of struggling with mud, bog, streamlets, and dicey fords, I see the river bend to the south and bend back north in a U shape: this must be Horseshoe Canyon. I spread my sleeping gear out on one side of the empty shelter and spend a pleasant late afternoon visiting the spring, listening to the river sounds mingle with the noise of a tributary brook, and savoring the prospect of a solitary night in this half wild forest.

Rain falls on and off all night, adding its patter to the other water sounds, and a light rain keeps up all morning as I walk the final nine miles back to Monson. In this part of Maine the usual granite gives way at times to slate bedrock, smoother and slipperier—I slide and fall hard on my butt three miles from the end, my one fall of this week long hike. Good to finally have that out of the way. One last crossing of the Piscataquis, this time the east branch, turns out to be only thigh deep, and before long the trail leads to the south, wilder end of Lake Hebron, then around it and over Buck Hill to the highway into Monson. I catch a ride to town with a woman who is just dropping off her son, another friendly, strong young thruhiker, at the edge of the 100 Mile Wilderness. In the car I tell her I will be following him north to Katahdin in one more year, pressing my hand down next to my thigh so she won't catch me crossing my fingers.

WINTER

Dew in the moonlight, a river of stars, snow-covered pines, clouds enveloping the peak.

Hongzhi Zhengjue, "Guidepost of Silent Illumination"

December 2007. The parking area is deserted as I sit at the edge of the passenger seat, the door open to the 20 degree chill, leaning over to lace up my boots. As I begin cinching my snowshoes over the boots a car pulls in and a middle-aged woman gets out, stares at me, and runs into the latrine as the driver idles, waiting. By the time I'm heading for the trailhead my car is the only one in the lot again. Not that surprising, given today's date: December 25th.

A gap of only 1.6 miles needs filling between the endpoints of two previous section hikes: straight up the north face of Moosilauke as far as Beaver Brook shelter, where I spent the night of my first AT out and back trip three years before. So, to keep things interesting, I've been saving this climb for a season of deep snow. The trail from the parking area has been broken out so the hike begins easily enough. Yet it looks like no one has come this way for at least a few days, as the sun has had time to round out the snowshoes tracks I follow. Soon I come to the big orange sign, just before the real climbing starts, there to warn off the uninitiated: "THIS TRAIL IS EXTREMELY TOUGH…TAKE SPECIAL CARE AT THE CASCADES TO AVOID TRAGIC RESULTS." And that's without accounting for two feet of packed snow over ice-glazed rock.

Unfazed, I follow the trail that climbs parallel to Beaver Brook, half frozen and gurgling icily in the gorge it cuts into the mountain just below me. At least I'm in no danger of losing the trail—between the snowshoe tracks, the brook, and the lack of anywhere else a trail could possibly be made. My first snowshoe hike, a year earlier, lacked all such orienteering advantages: I spent the first two hours floundering in deep snow after passively following the sole set of tracks up to what turned out to be a long abandoned ski area. Lesson one: someone else's tracks may be easy to follow and may also lead you miles from where you meant to go. Fortunately, lesson two taught me that however bewildered you get, unless it's snowing heavily you can always follow your own tracks back to where you got lost (and if it's snowing that heavily, you probably should have stayed home). After finding a white blaze at last I ended up snowshoeing less than half of the six miles I'd set out to cover, stopping when I reached a trail shelter that, unlike the usual three-sided variety, featured a fourth wall with glassed in windows and a sliding door and, even more unexpectedly, a wood stove with a provision of firewood piled neatly next to it. Feeling like I'd stumbled into a fairy tale hut in the woods I half expected a witch or a dwarf to come visit me after dark, but nothing more sinister than a hooting great horned owl came near that night in the Green Mountains.

Tonight, I know, will be different: a classic New Hampshire lean-to, open to the northeast, perched high on the mountainside a stone's throw from the brook that keeps me company as I hike. Assuming, of course, that I make it there. I have no worries about tragically sliding off the trail, no matter how icy it gets, at the cascades or anywhere else. My lightweight ice-axe stays ready in the grip of my gloved right hand, strapped to my wrist for extra security, and my muscles still remember the self-arrest routine I drilled into them decades earlier climbing glacial western peaks. Flip the axe up so the shaft lies directly across the chest, pick end forward, fall hard onto the ice or snowpack, driving the pick in, bend the legs up at the knees so a crampon tip doesn't catch before the axe and flip you head over heels. (Or, today, to get the snowshoes up and out of the way). And if the pick doesn't bite in right away, keep pushing down with all your strength and weight till it does.

The problem, rather, is that the Beaver Brook Trail really is extremely tough. In summer, some of the granite slabs on the way up angle so steeply that iron rungs have been driven into the rock as climbing aids. Now they remain invisible under a foot of hard, crusty snow. With the temperature hovering near 20 all afternoon, the snowpack refuses to soften, so I find it nearly impossible to kick my snowshoes into the slope when I reach one after another vertical or nearly vertical pitch. I should stop, take off my snowshoes, lash them to my backpack, and strap on my crampons, half dangling from a packloop in their nylon case. But the old stubbornness wells up and I become determined to climb this in low-budget snowshoes never intended for such a use. The head of my ice axe proves too light to chop steps into the steeper pitches, so I take to driving the shaft instead into the frozen slope just over my head, pulling myself up with it, then flailing around with my feet till the snowshoes find or make just enough purchase to hold me to a slow slide as I stab the axe in again a foot higher up, unless I slide all the way back down and have to start over again. Which can happen two or three times till at last I can get the pick onto some kind of ledge or shelf and chin myself over it like a sea lion bellying onto a rock. All the time I'm climbing this way my retro external frame backpack, loaded with forty pounds of winter gear, hangs from me like a deadweight determined to pull me over. Sweating in the frigid air I shed my parka and clip it to the packframe, where it swings back and forth and whips at my face whenever the wind picks up.

In short, I'm having the time of my life. The mountain positively vibrates with silence, cold, and solitude. My heaving gasps of air both burn and chill my lungs, my skin tingles under all my winter protection, my body and mind come together in a single shared focus, inching up the slope without sliding off it.

Whenever I stop to rest, as I do every few minutes, I pause to look around at the winter mountainscape. The brook cascades beneath me over glazed rocks and under half formed canopies of ice; bright flashes of sun on water contrast with the softer gleams of the ice and the tiny sparkles in the nearby snow. Away from the brook most of the rock lies buried under the snowpack and the whole mountainside shines in the sun. The fir and spruce trees take on deeper greens against the blanched snow beneath them and the dry, frigid air gives the sky an intense, austere blue.

A third of a mile short of the shelter turnoff the tracks I have been following give out, maybe drifted over, maybe because whoever made them decided they'd had enough and turned back. Either way I now move forward breaking trail, glad the steepest climbing is now behind me, grateful too for the white blazes that never fail, in contrast to the unevenly blazed section of trail I kept losing back in Vermont the winter before. I reach the side trail a little before four in the afternoon—it's taken me over three hours to climb a little over a mile and a half. I half walk, half surf through unbroken powder to the Beaver Brook shelter, unvisited for at least several weeks, and spread out my gear ten minutes before the early sunset begins.

I sit a while at the shelter edge watching the red and orange glow spread out over the snow-covered peaks of the Franconia Ridge across the Notch, until it's time to start preparing Christmas dinner. Oddly enough, I was supposed to be in Brazil today, where summer would have been in full swing and I most likely would have spent the morning at the beach in Copacabana or Ipanema with my Brazilian girlfriend, Marlena. But her extended visit to Boston the month before ended badly. Once I was certain I had to break things off and cancel my flight to Rio it was too late to book a trip to Seattle. With the kids away in San Francisco visiting their maternal grandparents, I had no reason to stay and spend a lonely holiday in my condo. So Christmas dinner, this year, will be a hearty two-serving packet of Mountain House freeze-dried beef teriyaki, with an appetizer course of half frozen baby carrots and a side of dried fruit. And boy am I hungry for it.

But as I unpack my small titanium cooking pot (with my smaller titanium backpacking stove nested inside it), I discover that I've somehow left my spoon, my sole backpacking utensil, on the counter at home. I mentally go through every item of gear in my backpack, trying to come up with some spoon-like item to no avail. And I can't think of an acceptable way to eat out of a resealable foil packet without one. Yet I'm counting on nearly every calorie I've brought with me to help me survive a sub-freezing night high up in the snowy mountains.

And then I see it. All around me stand evergreen trees and every one of them has branches covered with offshoots and twigs. One of these is a wooden spoon just waiting to be whittled into existence. Soon I'm digging into the spicy beef and rice and vegetables with a crude fir implement, more spade than spoon, that gives each bite an extra dash of resiny flavor. When it grows too dark to see my food I light the candle lantern instead of switching on my headlamp, wanting the softer light.

After I finish eating I'm cold enough—and tired enough—to consider getting into my sleeping bag, though it's not quite six p.m. But I can't tear myself away from the night sky now spread out before me. The first star out tonight is not Venus but a different planet, a fiery red one low on the horizon that must be Mars yet looks three times its normal size. I later learn that the red planet has swung unusually close to Earth, closer than it has for years. As I gaze at the huge red star, half mesmerized, more and more stars appear around it and above it, first singly, then in clusters, then at last the Milky Way, a vague river of stars stretching across the middle sky. A low band of clouds hugging the ridgeline under Mars starts filling with light as the moon, one day past the full, slowly emerges from behind it. Once the moon has broken free from the horizon it eclipses the Milky Way, but the snow covered mountains now gleam in the distance and the snowy slopes beneath me grow radiant, alive with a million frozen sparks of reflected moonlight.

I stay balanced on the edge of the open shelter, watching the ghostly vapor of my breath disperse into the air, the candle near me barely flickering inside its glass sheath. And then I remember it's time to break out my Christmas treat, a large Cadbury Fruit and Nut bar. I slowly eat the whole bar square by square, thawing it in my mouth, the flavors of chocolate and raisin and hazelnut mingling with the frigid bite of the air and the faint scent of balsam fir as I sit, under a cold moon, in the very heart of winter.

March 2009. To say I feel relieved to find hard-packed snow and a broken out trail would be an understatement. This is the fourth month in a row I've tried to snowshoe the 7.7 miles from the parking area on NH 302, across from the Webster Cliffs, to Zealand Falls Hut (where Nate and I ended the long AT part of our hut to hut traverse a few years back). In December, with two feet of snow on the ground, a freakish warm spell pushed the temperatures into the 50s during my holiday break and I held back, knowing that every slushy step would sink a foot deep. The one weekend I had free in January began with a classic Northeaster and it was all I could do that Saturday to shovel out my driveway: I needed my snowshoes just to get to the corner store. In February I managed to drive to the trailhead through a steady light snow, passing at least two crash sites on I-93 where cars had spun out and skidded off the highway.

That day I arrived at the trailhead to find ten to twelve inches of fresh powder on top of three feet of packed snow—the white blazes, level with the top of my head in summer, came to my knees. I followed the snowshoe tracks a pair of winter climbers had left to where the Willey Range trail breaks off, then had to break my own trail, at an arduous mile an hour pace, to just past Ethan Pond. I used my light ice axe as a probe (it telescopes out to make a walking staff), pushing the shaft through the powder to locate the harder packed snow of the beaten path beneath. Even so, I had fallen through where a hidden stream crossing the trail had undermined the snowpack from below, four feet down, and then struggled for fifteen minutes to climb back out with my backpack pulling against me and my snowshoes catching in the tumble of snow. Finally I lost the trail entirely, no blaze in sight, no resistance to my probe from below, with barely enough time to reach the Hut before dark *if* I found the trail again and *if* I didn't fall into another hidden stream or spruce trap. I had the sense to turn around and head for home.

Though three feet of snow still cover the ground (it has been another winter of near record snowfalls), today I find the path so well packed down by the hikers before me that I strap my snowshoes onto my backpack and stretch a pair of microspikes over my boots instead. I love this relatively new piece of gear, much lighter than full crampons but just as useful and dependable for most trail conditions, more packable too and much, much easier to get on. My bootsoles now armed with a dozen steel teeth, I move confidently over the snow, packed down so hard that at times the carbide tip of my extended ice axe barely punctures it. My speed doubles compared to last month's push through deep powder, back up to my usual two miles an hour, and the evergreen boughs no longer sag with loose snow that tumbles off as I brush past them and makes icy streamlets running down my back. Today the trees are only dusted with snow, just enough to give a midwinter look to the forest (though the calendar suggests spring should already have arrived). The temperature stays a few degrees under freezing, cold enough to keep the footing solid and warm enough to make for pleasant walking in a windshirt over a short-sleeved T. All of last month's tricky hazards—the hidden stream crossings, the spruce traps, the random soft patches—have been laid bare by previous hikers, leaving holes in the snowpack that make for easy, fun leaps. Yet the woods still look pristine and glistening and a very light snow continues to fall, adding fresh sparkles to this world of gleaming white and deep forest green.

Past Ethan Pond the solution to last month's mysteriously disappearing trail reveals itself. The path unexpectedly hooks left, away from the river it has been following, without the usual warning of a double white blaze. The next blaze in sight appears far off in the distance and only ten inches above the drifted snow—it must have been totally covered back in February. This time the trail stays easy to follow and the microspikes give me all the traction I need. Just one short jag, on an extremely narrow path across some ledges a mile south of the hut, gives me pause and makes me wonder if I should have brought full crampons as a backup. It proves treacherous but just passable. If it had iced over, my snow hike might have been cut short once again.

Instead, I find myself at the hut by two p.m., with a nice long afternoon ahead of me. The Zealand Falls, so pleasant in summer, have grown nothing short of spectacular over this long winter. The horizontal stretches over smooth rock, where Nate and I bathed after five days in the mountains, have become dense sheets of ice, riddled with cracks and bubbles that refract the sunlight, just now breaking through, in a thousand different ways. The cascades have frozen into crazy sculptures of snow-crusted ice, pierced by caves and hollows that make channels for the echoing sounds of water moving below. If the world looked transformed before, it looks enchanted, spellbound, now.

I return to the empty hut to warm up, read, and drink hot chocolate as a dozen or so winter backpackers begin to arrive in small groups. Though by now I can barely tolerate the huts in high season I actually like them when surrounded by snow. The youthful hut "croos" of half a dozen chirpy twenty-somethings give way to a single caretaker, sobered up by days at a time of snowbound isolation. No compulsory evening skits (compulsory if you want to stay for dessert, which you always do) about blanket folding and the like aimed at kids. For that matter, no blankets and, for the most part, no kids, though one intrepid young mom has pulled two young boys behind her on a sled five miles up Zealand Road (closed for the season) and the Zealand Trail. No prepared meals—we cook dinner in shifts in the large kitchen. In stark contrast to the summer crowds, no one who backpacks to the huts in winter complains about the trail or the conditions, because no one ever expected it to be easy. The colder and tougher the conditions get, the more the AMC huts return to being what they were originally meant to be: not Alpine-style inns catering to outdoorsy tourists, but spartan overnight refuges for backcountry adventurers.

The next morning the temperature unexpectedly plunges into the single digits and I leave the hut wearing pretty much every piece of cold weather gear I've brought: heavy weight zip-T, fleece-lined windshirt, winter parka, balaclava, neck gaiter, snow hat, windpants over winter hiking pants over long underwear bottoms, two layers of gloves, expedition weight socks under insulated boots. Again I just manage to scramble along the six-inch dent in the hard-crusted snow crossing the ledges, my light ice axe at the ready, and this time I succeed in following every white blaze, discovering a third of a mile of trail through a wooded field where the tracked snow veers too far to the right. I should stop and put on my snowshoes but, yet again, my stubborn streak wins out and I keep going, postholing through the deep snow, sinking in up to my thighs with each step, stupidly enjoying the challenge. Nearly exhausted, I plough through the last few yards to rejoin the hardened trail, further hardened by my own steps from the day before. And now I can get back to simply enjoying a long morning's walk in the bright snow.

January 2010. Another winter of surprise blizzards and heavy snowfalls starts early this year and, despite all the shoveling I've been doing since the early 1990s, I still love it. A Seattle childhood means rarely getting enough snow and hardly ever getting to fetch your trusty American Flyer sled from the attic. So the boy in me never tires of snowy New England winters and the grownup in me never tires of indulging him.

This snowhike nearly ends before it begins when I misread a sign in the Lafayette Campground parking area and drive my NewBeetle straight into a morass of deep snow. All my efforts to dig out fail, but half a dozen snowmobilers suddenly arrive out of nowhere and two of them dismount and trudge toward me when I wave them over. Their faces invisible beneath massive ski goggles and heavy balaclavas, the masked strangers push me out as I work the clutch and gas pedal. Then they roar back into the forest as I wave my gratitude; no word has ever been spoken between us. Never again will I feel even slightly irked at sharing the winter woods with snowmobilers.

Once more in silence and solitude I snowshoe up the Lonesome Lake trail, so well broken out and beaten down that I could probably switch to microspikes. But around the lake the snow has piled and drifted as high as two feet; only the snowshoes make walking possible now. I stop in the hut to drink hot water from the big urn in the kitchen—it's twenty degrees out and growing colder—and chat a little with a nice couple in for the night. The hut will serve as my failsafe option if I can't manage to stay on the trail to my destination: the Kinsman Pond lean-to two miles away and 1200 feet higher up the steep northern slope of the Kinsman Ridge.

Leaving the hut, I'm happy to discover a single set of snowshoe tracks heading up the AT, perhaps left by a winter climber "doing the grid"—that is, trying to bag all forty-eight of the New Hampshire four thousand footers in every month of the year. The tracks are barely drifted over and easy to follow, and though I do not pass quite as many reassuring white blazes as I would like (many have been covered over by light windblown snow), they do keep reappearing each time I worry the tracks may have veered astray. Soon the trail (here still called by its old local name, the Fishin' Jimmy Trail) angles dramatically up and my pace slows to a crawl. A literal crawl, at times, as I grasp at roots and tree trunks with both gloved hands while kicking in with my snowshoes, feeling all the weight of my backpack, inching up what must be near vertical slabs of rock. Only later do I learn that this section features a number of iron bars and even ladders nailed into the granite, otherwise impossible to scale without technical equipment. Today the ladders stay invisible under the snowpack and I climb like a bear or a raccoon, kicking and pulling and scratching my way up one wall of snow after another.

In a couple of places the tracks skew only a yard or less away from steep, icy precipices and I can only hope that the snow holds under me; if it gives way, I'm not certain that my ice axe will find anything firm enough to bite into before I go into a long, deathly slide down the near slope, dotted with the ice-glazed tips of granite crags projecting darkly from the snowcrust. Then the trail levels off some and I move more confidently for a while until, sooner than I would like, another long series of steep pitches begins. Where not so much as a sapling offers a handhold I need to rely on my ice axe again, shortening the staff and spiking it into the snowslope so I can hoist myself to where glove or snowshoe can find or force some kind of purchase. I check my watch—I left my car late, around noon—and promise myself that I will turn around and head for the hut if I haven't gotten to Kinsman Pond by 3:30—less than an hour before sunset.

At 3:15 I come to a "forest protection zone" sign, which tells me that the pond is only a quarter mile ahead. The side trail to the shelter is deeply buried under untracked snow, at least another foot more than the twelve inches of fresh powder that came down three days ago. It looks as though no one has visited the lean-to since early December, not a hiker, not a woodland creature, nothing but deep, fluffy, unblemished snow all around. The shelter, recently rebuilt, features a rare, partial fourth wall in front, with a big permanent opening like a missing barn door built into it. Still, snow has blown in and mostly covered the bare wood floor. Luckily, the loft above only has a dusting of powder, easily swept out with the shelter broom.

I cinch my snowshoes back on to walk down to the pond before the light fades. When I get to the edge my breathing slows and I stand motionless, entranced by the view before me and the vast stillness that surrounds me. Low clouds soften the winter light and give a slight blur to the distant slopes. The pond has frozen hard and cottony snow covers its entire surface, lending a soft texture to the pale light and giving off a dull glisten as the dusk sets in. The forests that ring the pond are so dense with snow cover that they make me think of a sheep's winter coat of fleece: thanks to days of subfreezing cold the powdery snow remains feather light and looks weightless on the evergreen boughs, unbent though as thickly laden with snow as they could possibly be.

Not a single track breaks the snow; not a single bird cuts the sky; not a breeze, not a sound anywhere. It all feels dreamlike, at once unreal and hyperreal, yet in a deeply quiet, infinitely calm way. I know in my heart and bones that at this moment I've become immersed in what the Zen ancestors call "the great silence." My breathing, the only motion in this motionless world, does not disrupt the stillness; my breathing *is* the stillness.

At some point the woods darken and I turn back toward the shelter, where I melt snow into simmering water I use to cook dinner with. I eat ravenously though I've only hiked four miles today: I've read somewhere that backpacking on snowshoes up a mountain through unpacked snow on a subfreezing day can burn a thousand calories an hour and tonight I believe it. I dine by candle lantern and then slither into my zero degree sleeping bag, a recent purchase, to read a book of short stories I've brought for the long evening ahead. The cold grows more intense as the night progresses until my little hiking thermometer reads 5 degrees, but I stay warm down to my toes in the winter bag. Before long I give up reading so I can pull the mummy hood more tightly around my face (already protected by a light balaclava), leaving only a small hole for the air to come through. When I wake up a few hours later my breathing hole has become a ring of ice, but the rest of the sleeping bag stays dry and keeps the chill out.

I expect that nightfall will only deepen the silence around me, if that is even possible. But the relatively new shelter pops and cracks all night with little settling noises, partly from the extreme cold, I guess, and partly from the snow load on the roof. And then some time after midnight I wake to hear a sound like thunder coming from the direction of the pond. At first I wonder if a great, ancient tree has fallen in the woods on the far shore, but at this elevation, nearly 4000 feet, the trees do not grow all that tall. Maybe a huge mass of snow has gone avalanching down the side of North Kinsman, somewhere far above me, or the steep slope of the ridge just below. Or, maybe, the pond itself is rumbling as some slight change in temperature triggers an invisible seismic shift in the thick sheet of ice that covers it. The last echoes die away and I drift back into sleep, happy to let the cause remain a mystery.

I stay in my sleeping bag till seven in the morning, warming my clothes by lying on them before putting them on, hoping in vain for the world outside to warm up as well. When I take one glove off to light the canister stove for breakfast something distracts me and by the time I go to light a match my right hand has gone totally numb and I cannot move so much as a finger. I work with my left hand, which is not much better, to pull a big insulated mitten over it, like trying to put a glove on a mannequin. Then I hug the frozen hand to my body, cradling it in my armpit, till it finally comes back to life with a long, agonizing burst of fiery tingles. It brings home to me how slender my safety margin is alone in the mountains in such bitter cold. But some risks are worth taking.

The light snow that began a few hours earlier continues to fall and the winter woods grow even whiter, fresher, more sparkly. I hike back down wondering, at the steepest parts of the trail, how I ever got up them. Every so often I go into a controlled skid in the thick, dry powder and ski a little on my snowshoes. The hut is empty when I stop in for hot chocolate and a Snickers bar and Lonesome Lake, frozen hard, lives up to its name as I hike back around it. At first I take my time, not wanting the solitude to end yet, but then I speed up, trying to get warm, moving quickly down the trail.

FALL (II)

For there is a path to follow, and there is walking to be done, and yet there is no walker.

Buddhaghosa, *Visuddhimagga*

October 2015. A cool morning, sunny with a frigid breeze. Having started out in a T-shirt and hiking gloves, I perversely refuse to stop and put on my windshirt as I cover the first couple of chilly miles through Damascus. My b&b stands right on the trail, a short walk from the Tennessee border where Jim McGavran met me at the end of a week-long section hike some years back. Now I'm heading north, along and across Laurel Creek, and then up a sharp climb that at last restores my body warmth, the trail rising 2500 feet over a series of picturesque hills with picturesque names like Cuckoo Knob and Straight Mountain. I stop for the night at Lost Mountain, a dozen miles short of the summit of Mount Rogers, the highest point in Virginia.

It's the first of 26 days on the Appalachian Trail and already I feel at home in the woods again, despite a groggy start after a night of drinking beer in town with my brother and some friendly locals. The cool air clears my head and the first fifteen miles go by quickly. I hike up the unusually smooth path, clear of all but the smallest stones, through a mix of oaks, maples, and what look like dogwoods, the leaves already gone bright red though it's only the first week of October. Higher up, following a series of long, loping switchbacks, I smile to find myself in a pine grove—all evergreens remind me of home. In between stands of pine the trail winds through long stretches of laurels and rhododendrons.

Sun splashes through pines,
rhododendrons line the path:
cold October day.

Most of my southern hikes have begun in May and I wait in vain for the remembered calls of towhees, wood thrushes, warblers, and ovenbirds. Instead I listen to the light percussion of acorns dropping from the tall oaks onto the forest floor, already half covered with fallen leaves. At Lost Mountain I share the campsite with a growing band of hikers, having passed almost no one all day. A junco hops around in front of the shelter, looking for crumbs, and I fall asleep under a big moon to the sound of acorns pattering and trees rustling in a breeze that never lets up.

No thrushes singing
but here a dark-eyed junco
flits white tail feathers.

I see juncos nearly every day over the course of the hike, in the woods, near the shelters, in the low bushes lining higher ridges. I also see or hear, by the time I reach Rockfish Gap, ravens, crows, and vultures, bluejays and mourning doves, flickers and downy woodpeckers, grouse flushed from steep mountain sides, chickadees and titmice, a brown creeper and a nuthatch working opposite sides of the same wormy oak tree, and a great horned owl calling out in the night.

The next day starts sunny and cool again, perfect weather for more easy climbing. The first five miles or so lead up to Buzzard Rock and soon after the summit of Whitetop, with the first expansive views of the hike.

One hundred mountains
in fall tones: deep reds, russets.
Feeling far from home.

I stay above 4500 feet for the rest of the day, watching birches, maples, and hemlocks grudgingly make room for spruces and firs as the trail rises toward Mt. Rogers. A short day (twelve miles), babying my feet, and just avoiding a thunderstorm that I see coming in fast from the short side trail up to the top of Rogers. Abandoning the summit attempt, I half run to the Thomas Knob shelter, reaching it just in time to fill my water bottles in the nearby spring and duck back in as the rainfall hits, hard. Two women with two big dogs and a small toddler between them decide to head back through the downpour, the little girl looking out from the hood of her tiny pink parka unfazed by the sheets of rain. Then I settle in, dry and happy, as the storm rages on. One by one most of the crew from the night before draggles in, dripping and clammy, and I try both not to feel guilty and not to feel smug as the rain flows in sheets off the eaves.

The next morning the rain has lightened enough for another dash to the spring, fenced off by a kind of corral, something I've never seen in the mountains before. We cook breakfast over tiny stoves and finish with a "leave no trace" cleaning ritual that resembles the bowl washing at the end of oryoki, formal meal practice at Zen retreats:

We scrape out our pots,
add rinse water, drink that too—
nothing gets wasted.

I'm first out of the shelter as the others wait for the light rain to end. But I'm eager to start this day. I walk the high country, mist clinging to my rain jacket. Here above 5000 feet the leaf change has already begun to peak. Low berry bushes with red leaves and bright red stems line the trail, now overlaid with yellow, red, and orange leaves. Grey and grey-green volcanic rock, hard as granite but finer grained, gleams wetly, fresh looking though 600 million years old. Among patches of rock, dark green mosses beneath dark green spruces mingle with yellow-leaved birch trees. Flanking the trail, hugging the rocks, little fields of thick, hay-like grass, running from green to ochre to burnt sienna. I barely notice when the rain lets up.

Now the trail climbs steadily over bare rock, just gritty enough to give decent footing. At the top of a small knob I get my first view of distant mountains to the north, mountains I'll scale over the next week or so, looming in and out of low clouds. The sun appears as a pale, moon-like disc behind the mist, the nearer hills show bands of leaf change—more reds, ochres, and golden yellows, dotted with lingering greens. Below the rocks and running between lines of hills, I see a high table land, covered with the same hay-like grass, but here shorter, looking almost mown.

I hear them before I can see them. A series of high, shrill calls, with a melodic contour that reminds me of laughing gulls, yet definitively horsey in timbre. A few steps higher and I can glimpse their hindquarters retreating into the woods, dappled black and white, with long, unkempt tails. At last I've seen the famous wild ponies of the Grayson Highlands, though I'm not yet through the stile that marks the boundary of their official preserve. Taking in the hills, the fields, the rocks, the blue mountains, the whinnying of the ponies, and the beating of my own heart, I'm surprised to hear myself saying, "Jesus."

And pausing to savor the view, I think I know why. What I'm seeing, what I'm feeling, taking in, letting myself become a part of, is what the ancient Chinese poets I've brought to read on this hike call "Tao," and by the same token what the ancestral Zen teachers I've been studying for the past decade call "Buddha" or "Buddha mind." And for the first time I understand how close this is to what my late friend and colleague Bob Barth, S.J., used to call, in talking of the Romantic poets we both loved, a "sacramental" vision of the world. This is my body.

Picking my way down the rocks to the long stretch of pasture land, I soon see the first two of a long line of wild ponies, on a beaten path a few hundred yards to my left, heading south as I head north. I've never seen horses sporting such a crazy, random mix of colors, white heads on brown bodies, black heads on white bodies, chestnut or coppery red torsos with white flanks, long untended manes, long uncropped tails. The ponies in the rear canter to catch up to the rest, who seem focused but unhurried.

Wild ponies amble
down a trail of their own making.
I amble past them.

On entering the Highlands proper you pass a sign that asks you not to feed the ponies, admonishing: "keep the wild in wildlife." Now feeling a deep kinship with these domestic creatures gone happily feral, I mentally add another line: "reclaim the wild in yourself."

And soon enough I'm reminded, yet again, of the difference between wildness and wilderness. Though originally imagined as a wilderness trail, the AT in fact runs through farmlands as well as federally protected wilderness areas, sometimes crossing a pristine subalpine meadow, sometimes a busy highway (I'll cross over or under major interstates three times on this long hike). Descending from the Highlands, I find myself walking an easy, horse-graded trail—Virginia is the only state where equestrians share stretches of the AT with hikers. The path cuts through cattle fields as well, including one occupied by a herd of placid but scary looking long-horned hybrids, with no fence to separate us. Then the trail runs directly past the Scales, a historic corral where Virginia ranchers once brought their horses and cattle for sale. Hiking past the wild ponies earlier, I'd been struck by the familiar feel of the topography, and suddenly realized where I'd seen the same contour lines of hill, pasture land, and distant mountains before, though in drier, dustier tones: Montana. That's when I first spot cattle grazing in the hills to the west. Cowboy country, eastern style.

A night of big winds brings a temporary change in the weather and I start out again under gradually clearing skies. Two nights of heavy rain have given the trail some much needed moisture—not long before, southbound hikers brought rumors of water sources giving out—though the ground has built up such a thirst that there's not a speck of mud on my boots.

The next few days stay clear and pleasant as I hike at lower elevations, descending into gaps, hiking back up the long, lazy switchbacks to pleasant ridges. More running water here—rills and streams and even a little cascade or two. More critters as well—up to now, aside from the odd chipmunk or red squirrel, I've only seen horses, cows, and a tiny shelter mouse. Now I step over a huge speckled wood frog and, climbing out of a gap, scare up as many as a dozen ruffed grouse, taking off with the little sonic booms they make, their broad tails spread wide as they vanish over the side of the ridge. Frogs and crickets sing at night as acorns and leaves fall with gentle percussive sounds. The rocks change as well, quartzite, sandstone, limestone, all in different pastel shades—the top of High Point, in the Iron Mountains, looks like a prehistoric rock garden.

I make my first town stop of the trip in Marion, showering, making up for lost calories, sleeping in an actual bed, and wake up early, reaching the trailhead in the dark. I near the top of Brushy Mountain just as the sky begins to redden in earnest and the whole forest flushes with it, the colored leaves underfoot glowing surreally with the rosy light. Then the sun breaks out over the ridge and the red light turns a rich golden, incredibly lovely, as the glowing light reflects upward from the forest floor to the green and yellow leaves clustered above me. The loud cry of a raven.

Red light drenches
the leaf scatter underfoot,
then the sun's gold glow.

Following the trail up and down as it roller-coasters over several more peaks, I see rain coming in from the west over a long line of mountains, a thick curtain of it, and the sky darkens again. I descend into another succession of fields and pastures, separated by narrow bands of woods and marked off by a variety of stiles I pass through, around, or over. Coming out of one field, I'm surprised to find myself facing an 1892 one room schoolhouse, the Lindamond School, A-frame design, weathered grey boards, the door open. Peeking inside, assuming it's a kind of museum, I see both the original nineteenth-century wooden forms and a group of children sitting in them, taking their lessons.

Back in the woods, I pass more schoolchildren wearing thin yellow throwaway raincoats, on their way to visit the antique schoolhouse as well. A friendly young Appalachian Trail Conservancy volunteer walking behind them gives me a taste of "autumn olives," a poisonous-looking red berry growing wild here, tasting like tart grapes with a hint of sour cherry. She tells me how to identify the bushes when I come to them, adding that they're "invasives." I almost ask, like us? I walk on as the rain comes down more heavily, wood sounds mingling with the noise of the highway and the railway crossing up ahead.

Walking in fall rain
through mountain laurel tunnels,
a train's low whistle.

As I near I-81 and the rain gets only heavier, a motel just 100 yards off the trail grows irresistible and I make it a short day, stopping at a nearby diner for a hamburger and at a gas station mini-mart for a six pack of Yuengling. My guilt fades the next morning when I hike past my intended campsite, perhaps the dreariest and most sinister looking I've ever encountered on the AT. First, though, I cross under I-81, after slipping on the wet grass leaving the motel (I'll fall twice more today).

Twice my path crosses
I-81, that brought me
here: part of the Trail.

The day never seems to break and I hike in dim light, but the wetness has brought dozens of scents into relief, gamy and earthy along the ridges, fruity and sweet near the bottoms, mixed with notes of compost, humus, and what Pinot Noir enthusiasts call "barnyard." I leave that night's shelter, Knot Maul Branch, early the next morning for my first long (19 mile) day—my feet are still 100%, though I've developed a tight, nagging knot behind my right shoulder that sometimes makes it hard to sleep. The day starts with a 1500 foot climb and then a long, long summit walk on Chestnut Knob, back above the 4000 foot elevation line and so dense with mist that you can barely see the widely spaced posts that mark the path over thick, wet, recently cut grass. Then come two ridges that go on for miles through low clouds.

Hiking this long ridge,
fine views: dense mist to the west,
to the east, dense mist.

I walk in solitude, passing no one the entire day, though I begin encountering the first few of a long succession of white-tail deer (also called "Virginia deer"), the does skittish and quick to run off, the yearling bucks, with small curved antlers, gamely standing their ground for a long minute before leaping away from the trail. The next morning the skies half clear and the woods reveal a lovely new shade of fall foliage.

On Brushy Mountain
the leaves turn a new color:
flesh of pink grapefruit.

I pass only one other hiker all day, although I hear bow hunters in the woods making bad impressions of wild turkey calls. Time to put on my blaze orange cycling cap. I sleep in a shelter a third of a mile off trail, surrounded by narrow trunked trees with branches too small or too high for hanging food. But with the hunters out, I expect the bears to stay put for the night and I let my food sack dangle from a bent nail on a roof beam.

And then a wild day: rainstorms threatening, winds gusting, trees and branches falling, water flowing, and me moving through it all and moving fast.

I'm aiming to hike 18 miles and then camp out in my tent. The various southbounders I meet, though, all talk about a torrential thunderstorm scheduled to hit—when? That's the point they disagree on, and I get opinions ranging from an hour from now (whenever now happens to be) to dusk. Meanwhile the winds are raging and I keep moving, listening to each cracking sound in the branches overhead, wary of mast-high evergreens that wave back and forth like palm trees in a hurricane.

The big winds up here
make even the tallest trees dance—
image of the mind.

Tempestuous weather or not, I'm on a beautiful stretch of smooth, friendly trail, colored leaves and brown pine needles under foot, hours of ridge walking with short rocky passages near the height of land, laurel canyons leading down to dirt or gravel roads, easy switchbacks leading back up to the ridge. I quickly stop worrying about the storm and enjoy the boisterous, outrageous energy of the day, feeling it pulse through my body. I seem to be alone in this—one southbounder can't wait to get off the ridge, certain that lightening will start stalking him any moment, though I look at the 50-foot trees that line both sides of the trail and wonder how the bolts would even find him. Another couple holes up at Jenny Knob shelter, which I reach by eleven in the morning, having covered a good ten miles in four hours. Feeling dubious that my ultralight tent can stand up in winds like these, I begin to think of making this a twenty-four mile day, so I can take refuge in the next lean-to if the coming storm does prove overpowering. The three-sided trail shelters may be open to the elements, but they rarely blow away in the wind.

After fifteen miles of fast hiking, with only a half hour break at Jenny Knob, I drift into a zone, like a runner's high but dreamier. Coming down a hillside toward broad Kimberley Creek I'm confronted, unaccountably, by a vertical wall of brownish water, which just as suddenly shifts it's orientation and becomes a horizontally flowing river. Crossing over on a suspension bridge I begin to see the bridge flow underfoot while the creek swirls in one place, weirdly like a famous Zen "enlightenment" poem:

Walking over a bridge,
The bridge flows, the water does not flow

Of course, in my case the narrow, bouncy bridge really is moving, and I see Kimberley Creek flowing again almost as soon as it seems to whirlpool in place. Nothing special. But with the winds howling away, the skies continually about to open up, and yet the rain always holding off, the day remains extraordinary and I stay in whatever altered state of mind I have stumbled, or hiked, my way into. The terrain I pass through completely fills my mind, streaming clouds, bending trees, swollen brooks, leaves and sticks and pebbles underfoot, and for the last few miles I chant Zen sutras, maybe to keep my energy up, maybe because they just want to be chanted. I reach Wapiti Shelter after eleven hours of walking, tired and exhilarated and hungry as a bear.

The promised storm hits about the time the few of us in the shelter have finished dinner, hard and heavy, rain spattering a foot into the open front—we squeeze toward the back wall. For the third time in a week, a hiker I've never met before offers me cannabis, this time in the form of a hashish pipe made from buckhorn. For the third time I pass, though perhaps it would help me sleep.

First one out in the morning, I take my boots off minutes after I've put them on to ford a series of rain swollen creeks. The cold, clear brook water, flowing through the holes in my Crocs and reaching as high as mid-calf, jolts me awake and chases the ache of yesterday's twenty-four miles out of my feet. Then back into hiking boots to climb another 1500 feet up Sugar Run Mountain. After a four mile ridge walk and a slight descent into a high brushy gap, I find hiker paradise half a mile off the Trail, just down Sugar Run Road.

Woods Hole Hostel consists of a antique farmhouse partly built from logs, a smaller log bunkhouse to one side, a chicken house, duck pen, hog pen (these hogs are HUGE), sheds, compost bins, and fenced in gardens. I'm greeted, successively, by two large dogs of indeterminate breed, two big farm cats, and the two two-legged hosts, Michael, a lean and darkly handsome former AT thru-hiker, and Neville, the fair haired and fair featured granddaughter of the farm's last owner. I take a shower, do my small load of laundry, and glug down a twenty ounce strawberry milkshake that, finally, eases the hunger that's been dogging me since the day before. Later I'll help Neville in the kitchen, preparing a simple, scrumptious vegetarian feast we share with Michael and a dozen or so hikers, featuring two of the foods we crave most, a huge bowl of fresh greens and limitless slices of home-baked bread. But not before I've taken a nap in the house (I've sprung for a private room) and gotten some temporary relief for the aching knot in my back (I've also sprung for one of Neville's famous therapeutic massages).

This was the hike I was determined to get right. After years of resisting, I'd abandoned my old-school Kelty Tioga for a high-market, twenty-first century internal frame backpack, one that seemed able magically to reduce the load on my back in half. I'd switched out my heavy Nalgenes for SmartWater bottles at a price of under five dollars; I'd also invested hundreds in newer, lighter incarnations of tent, air pad, even stuff sacks. My base pack weight, before I'd added in food and water, was now a modest nineteen pounds. Just in time to break them in, I bought new, lighter boots, mid-weight with mesh-paneled uppers, easier on the feet and equivalent to taking several additional pounds off my back. I'd done a series of practice overnights, not to mention a week in the Maine mountains, and hardened my feet to the point that, in 390 miles, I never developed so much as a hot spot let alone the blisters that had plagued me on earlier "long" hikes. I'd planned what turned out to be a perfect buildup, followed by just the right combination of longer and shorter days. I'd arranged a maildrop at least every five or six days so I never had to carry much more than 30 pounds.

Life, though, has other things on its mind than respecting our plans. Walking from my motel in Marion to a local watering hole, five days into my hike, my back seizes up in a cruel knot, just behind my right shoulder. Over the next week I try rebalancing the packload and adjusting the straps multiple times but the pain just gets worse. It's not too bad while I'm hiking, which makes it at least preferable to foot problems, but soon I can't sleep either on my right side or on my back, which means trying to get through long nights with my left side aching from the unrelieved hardness of the ground or shelter floor pressing through a thin ultralight pad. I'm usually exhausted enough to sleep for the first few hours, but I wake often and find myself giving up each morning while the stars are still shining. In the hostel, on a soft bed, for once I'm able to sleep on my back again. At 3 a.m. one of the farm cats, a dingy white, fluffy Abyssinian mix, leaps up to join me.

Neville had worked for an hour trying to untangle my upper back muscles but can offer no theory as to what's been traumatizing them. I leave before breakfast the next morning, descend into the charmless industrial town of Pearisburg, which gives off a noxious mix of chemical odors, and work my way back up to the next ridge, a twenty mile day. The trail out of Pearisburg is brand new—smooth, graded, and nearly broad enough to drive a jeep up. It has recently been relocated around a massive gas pipeline project, one of several I encounter in Virginia, and looks as though it was planned by soil engineers and not trail builders. At the top, Rice Field Shelter indeed faces out onto a pretty field, though Rice must have been the name of the farmer and not the crop. The blue silhouettes of the West Virginia Appalachians rise far over the fields. At night I hear the muted voices of pipeline workers in their trailers, and from a little rise on the way to the privy I can see the stadium lights of a construction site.

The distant howling of coyotes wakes me and I'm off again in the halflight of early morning. It's prime walking on a high, wide ridge, through forgotten fields and abandoned orchards. Ripe apples have dropped to the ground and I find a perfect one next to the trail. It's some local heirloom variety I've never seen before, shaped like a Macintosh but greenish yellow, with a roughish skin like a Bosc pear. It tastes tart and appley, and I devour it right to the inner core. It's the most delicious piece of fruit I've ever eaten.

Around ten the sun comes out and then the skies clear completely—the first unblemished blue since the beginning of my hike almost two weeks earlier. Enjoying the fields, the woods, and the cool October sun, I indulge in little breaks, partly to get the pack off my back—which now hurts even when I walk. I make another, longer stop and inspect the pack once again, checking its balance, looking hard at every strap, adjusting and readjusting. Then for the first time I notice the hydration sleeve, stretched across the back panel of the pack, where it hugs my shoulders. I slide my hand inside and find an eight-inch twig, ending exactly in the spot where I first noticed the pain. I guess that it slid into the sleeve when I was squeezing under a blowdown during one of the early, blustery days, and then snapped off, hidden and unsuspected. Based on when the pain started, I calculate that it's been digging into my back for 150 miles, pressed in by the twenty-five to thirty pounds I'm always carrying.

I fling the twig away but the damage is done. Knowing I can't take the days off the trail I'd need to start healing, I reconcile myself to more troubled nights, though quite soon I am again walking without pain. Fair enough. It's now the thirteenth of twenty-six days on the trail, with something over two hundred miles to go.

From now on most days include sixteen to twenty miles of backpacking, often with elevation gains of 3000, 4000, or (once) close to 5000 feet. Every so often a shorter or flatter day provides just enough respite. Luckily, the fine weather holds: one journal entry after another from this period reads "perfect hiking weather," "sunny, blue skies," "sunny and cold." After all the rain early on, the streams and springs run fast and clear. Water crossings become more frequent, always dry-booted, over rocks or wooden bridges or across narrow channels taken with a short leap.

The path grows rockier and the ascents steeper. The trail climbs a series of famous high points, ones I've heard other hikers talk about for years: Dragon's Tooth, McAfee Knob, Spy Rock. The first and last involve an almost Maine-worthy level of rock scrambling; all three open up expansive views (yet another reason to bless the clear skies). Each one, along with many other views from the higher ridges, provides a variation on a now familiar theme: lovely farm and pasture land in the valleys below, bordered by rivers and streams, hills just beyond in peak foliage colors, russet, yellow, red, orange, oxblood, yellow-green; golden brown foothills further away; lines of dim blue mountain ranges further still.

I splurge on another hiker oasis, Huffman House, run by perhaps the sweetest elderly couple I can remember ever meeting. After the usual long shower is over, they drive me to what must be the best restaurant in the Appalachians, Palisades, and then get up before sunrise to cook me a titan's breakfast and drop me at the trailhead in time to start a twenty-mile day in early light. (The mid-October sun rises a little after seven.) I hike a long, long rocky ridge that morning, dotted with the relics of stone pens or huts—for sheepherding? Or some crop that only grew in high places? Long views open up, first on one side of the ridge and then the other, and near the height of land I feel that I'm treading the petrified spine of the whole grand Appalachian system, with wave after wave of mountain ranges to both east and west. Just minutes later I come up on a sign marking the Eastern Continental Divide. Naturally I stop to pee on both sides, one stream running toward the Atlantic seaboard, the other toward the Gulf of Mexico. I imagine it's something Walt Whitman would do: I stride continents, my pee roils the oceans.

Another mountain and another long ridgewalk later, I hike down through thin, feathery pine trees to a sweet hollow with a pretty, clear running creek at the very bottom. (I mostly drink untreated water on this hike, with no ill effects.) It's quiet and removed, a bit off trail, and I explore the dell, listening to breezes, leafdrop, and birdcalls until a young, long-haired Floridian, Spirit Walker, who reminds me of the hippie chicks of my own youth, shows up in time for dinner. She tells me, very sincerely, how she saw a mountain lion in Shenandoah National Park and I let it pass, though I'm certain it must have been a bobcat. I like talking with Spirit Walker; I enjoy her open heart and easy presence. We laugh together a lot, telling trail stories, then fall asleep at opposite ends of the shelter as coyotes sing eerily somewhere in the woods behind us.

The next day I hike seventeen miles and again gain well over 3000 feet, first up the Dragon's Tooth, then ups and downs over the aptly named Sawtooth Ridge, then a big climb to McAfee Knob, with perhaps the longest views of the hike. Somewhere along the way I see a lizard on the trail—I've seen dozens of snakes, frogs, and toads and hundreds of salamanders on the AT but I can't remember ever seeing a lizard. The morning after, my upper back still feels fine during the day but all of my trail muscles are aching—my calves, my upper thighs, my lower back, my hips, even my abdominals—and oh my aching feet. But so what? It's yet another cool, sunny day and I'm covering just over fifteen miles, which now feels like a short day. Hiking along Tinker Ridge, en route to a second crossing of I-81, I'm again struck by how the Appalachian Trail laces together the wild and the urbane, the green world and concrete.

Walking Tinker Ridge,
to east: factories, trains, highways;
to west: the long, still lake.

After composing this haiku, I discover that the sparkling, serpentine lake I've seen from high up is in fact a reservoir. We can draw lines between nature and culture; we just can't expect them to stay put.

After a town stop in Daleville, just off the highway, featuring the usual shower, maildrop, and calorie splurge, I do a short day to Wilson Creek shelter where I find myself alone for the night—something that happens more often now. I can barely hear an occasional car passing by somewhere well above me; I look at the map and find out I'm a few miles from the Blue Ridge Parkway. But by early evening the traffic has quieted and, for once, I decide to build a small campfire. The campsite is perched on a low, wooded hill and there are twigs and branches everywhere on the ground, ripped from the trees above by weeks of high winds. As I sit by my fire, two deer, a doe and fawn, walk along the trail not twenty yards from the shelter. They stop and regard me as I regard them by the light of my headlamp in the thickening dusk. The doe stays for ten minutes or longer, staring intently.

Far from the roadways
in a headlamp's thin beam,
a deer stands transfixed.

When she at last moves off, snapping twigs underfoot as she goes, I let the campfire die down, watching the color drain from the fall leaves and the high ridge above me meld with the darkening sky.

The mountain goes dark
against a campfire's embers;
red leaves dim to black.

In the days to come the AT stays linked in a pas de deux with the Blue Ridge Parkway, sometimes running parallel to it, sometimes crisscrossing it, occasionally careening away for miles only to rejoin it later. I find the Scenic Parkway decidedly less scenic than the wilder ridges further south, but the trail mostly stays out of sight of the roadway and the crossings, often featuring bear-proof trash bins, provide a chance to lighten the packload a bit. Now the high winds return with a vengeance, threatening a change in the weather that never comes, and again I feel caught up in the dynamic energy of a landscape set into wild motion.

A wind to beat all
winds: the Blue Ridge comes to life
as trees reel, leaves swirl.

This last long week on the trail takes on a character of its own. The sun now sets before 6 p.m. and sleep usually takes me by 8. Waking before 4 in the morning, for the first time I take to hiking in the dark, starting the day in starlight, picking the trail out with the meager glow from my headlamp. I'm struck with how intimate this feels, first because I'm moving along in such a narrow circle of light, but also because I rely on my entire body to stay on the path.

Hiking by headlamp
ears, toes, stick hand all alert,
a small pool of light.

Sometimes my feet know that I'm veering off trail before my eyes do; I can hear and even smell little streams coming up well before I see them. I use my hiking staff almost like a blind man using a cane, prodding ahead for loose rocks or boggy spots. Hands and feet together find out the sharp turns in hiking up switchbacks.

Switchbacks in the dark:
feel the hard dirt underfoot,
turn when you hit rock.

I click my headlamp off as soon as the dawn starts to glimmer, wanting to prolong the sense of intimacy a bit longer.

And then I get to savor every phase of sunrise, as shadows begin to detach themselves from the mass of darkness around me and the greyish rocks, then the tree trunks, and finally the dark evergreen boughs slowly reveal their daytime colors. Stars dim and then vanish into a gathering tide of pale sky-blue, first singly and then in waves, while streaks of pink and orange bleed onto the horizon; low clouds take on gilded undersides. The visible surround expands again as distances open up and objects reassert their edges: the world grows larger and more definite. And at last, maybe after an hour of steady brightening, the sun shows its liquid rim over a nearby mountain top or ridge line, rising quickly as though eager to lift free of the earth. Through some unaccountable alchemy this happens every morning.

As the days grow shorter and colder I pass fewer hikers and more white tailed deer. So different from my earlier May hikes the in south, when I would chance upon little stands of wild orchids and walk past literally thousands of mountain laurel, rhododendron, and wild azalea blooms, I've seen few flowers since leaving Damascus. Red and yellow leaves have taken the place of pink and flame-colored petals. But hiking out of Wilson Creek, where I'd communed over a dying fire with a deer and her fawn, right beside the trail I see something lovely and unaccountable, a single iris in full bloom. It seems impervious to the cold and wind, unconscious of how far out of season it has chosen to unfold.

A sole dwarf iris
under cold October skies,
perfect and serene.

A day after seeing the iris I climb three separate mountains, each of respectable size, gaining some 4800 feet in one day, and yet I do not get tired or slow down. Reaching camp, even my back feels better and I sleep unusually well, waking up only when a bobcat begins screaming some time after midnight. I've been on the trail for three weeks now, building stamina, consolidating muscle, losing weight—at least ten pounds. I take pleasure in the efficient, resilient, vibrant feel of my body. Though I'm a year away from 60, age has for the time pulled back, like the ocean pulling away from the shore before crashing back even higher a few wave cycles later. For now, I feel invincible. And very, very hungry.

This is the long distance hiker's paradox: the more food I carry the more calories I burn, and apart from town stops my bodily economy is running at a steady loss. I try to stay with the trail, loosely focused on whatever I happen to encounter—switchbacks, sunrises, rocks, tricky descents on slippery leaves, vistas, streams, gravel—and I find myself thinking about food for hours on end. Mostly about what I'll get at the next town or campground: ice cream, peanut butter crackers, Snickers bars, potato chips, fresh fruit, beer. All of which I eagerly consume, along with any salads, burgers, and fries on offer, and then carry extra snacks with me for the next couple of days in the woods.

In my last week on the trail, two nights spent alone stand out most vividly, each connected to a different aspect of what I've come to love about the AT—the way it tangles up with human history, and the way it asserts a vein of wildness in the midst of human encroachment. Both nights come at the end of tough, satisfying eighteen-mile days with ample climbing. To reach Brown

Mountain Creek I start early, hiking 1400 feet out of John's Hollow to reach the first viewpoint on the ridge, Fullers Rock, just in time for sunup. By 10:30, summiting Bluff Mountain at the height of another long ridgewalk, I've already gained close to 3000 feet, with a few hundred more to come as smaller climbs break the long descent. At last I come to the prettiest of several very pretty brooks I've hiked along over the past week or so. I follow Brown Mountain Creek slightly uphill as it transforms from a broad, sleepy valley stream to a half sparkling, half shaded succession of cascades, shallow pools, multiple streamlets edging around large, smooth boulders, and short stretches of glassy water flowing over beds of pebbles and dark green moss. All along, on the far side of the creek, I keep spotting remnants of rock walls and structures, widely spaced, screened by bushes and slender trees. A sign on the side of the trail tells me that I'm traveling through the site of a nineteenth century free Black community. I can understand the appeal of this site for anyone who wanted to at last live freely, though I can't imagine what all could be cultivated or manufactured in this wildish place. Later I learn that most of the settlers were sharecroppers, growing corn and tobacco and oats. Some were named Richardson, like me, descendants of a white slaveholder and one of his female slaves. But I can claim no blood relation: my Richardson forbears came from Scotland, through Canada, well after the Civil War.

To reach the lean-to I cross the creek to the far side, but now well above where I spotted the ruins. No one is here. I set up and scramble back down the steep bank to the smooth rocks that line the river. I take off my camp shoes and plunge both feet into the water, keeping them there till they're almost numb with cold. They tingle as I dry them with a thin strip of packtowel. I spread out the toes and wiggle them up and down, flexing my whole foot, then rest and try to commune with the ghosts downstream—to no avail. There's nothing remotely supernatural about the night to come—just stream sounds, water rushing and splashing a few yards below me, and a breeze cool enough to make my sleeping bag cozy—I pull the mummy hood close around my face. I sleep well but not too long, back on the trail again in starlight.

My last full day on the trail comes as close to perfect as I could want it to be. I'm not hungry, having raided the little store at lovely Crabtree Falls campground the evening before—the very hip former hiker who runs it even did a beer run into town for me. Dave also drives me back to the trailhead at first light—I had hitched to Crabtree the afternoon before, passed by numerous

Audis and Priuses and finally picked up by a friendly, dissolute looking local with an unkempt, tobacco-stained beard, a twinkle in his blue eyes, and a confederate flag stretched over his pickup's rear window. We talked about the local terrain. He filled me in on the Civil War history of Spy Rock. (It offers long views on every side and proved a perfect spot to scope out the approach of Yankee soldiers coming from any direction whatsoever.)

Hiking out of the Tye River valley looks tough on the map—three serious ascents in close succession, a good 3000 feet of climbing up to the high point (at almost 4000 feet) of the Three Ridges. On the trail, it feels great—each climb ends in a little break, a bit of down but not so much you feel you're losing too much of the ground you've just gained. Views open up at each stage, the Tye River flashing with the sun as it runs along the valley floor, bisecting what looks from high up like a huge cirque, the still green pasture lands rimmed with red and yellow and orange leaf change, the whole framed by mountains clothed in a warm russet as the fall colors blend in the distance.

The trail then leads gently down through pleasantly named landmarks—Bee Mountain, Maupin Field, Meadow Mountain—till it stretches out along a level, featureless ridge, the trail running parallel below the height of land, often approaching the ridgetop only to veer slightly down again. In a narrow vale below a hound bays remorselessly, seemingly for hours—troubled, perhaps, by the sound of my footsteps far above him. I stop at an unmarked spring, gushing out of the mountainside, and fill my water bottles. The two advertised springs I pass later both prove to be muddy holes.

Testing my legs against the final climb of the day, some 800 feet up Humpback Mountain, I find myself dwelling on a southbounder's story about the terrain ahead. He'd shambled into camp a few nights back, a huge unwieldy pack on his back, a sleeping bag hanging from the bottom, a big tarp lashed crookedly to the top, a plastic grocery bag (which turned out to hold a loaf of sliced bread) swinging from the side. Turtle has done well enough with his own landscaping outfit to leave his favorite employee, his father, in charge of the business while he tries backpacking the Blue Ridge area. A classic newbie, he hikes just five to eight miles a day—I admire his willingness to go slow and roam the bypaths even while I notice the squirrels diving for the breadbag that's now dangling from the packframe he's somehow slung up over a tree branch that bends under its weight. He tells me he learned a lesson camping at a picnic area on a Blue Ridge Parkway pull off, at Humpback Mountain, when he set up his tent too close to a large trash bin. Sitting at the picnic table he watched a bear approach, sniff at his tent, and then proceed to rip it apart. All good, Turtle adds; he really prefers sleeping under his tarp.

Humping up Humpback, a little spent from the morning's triple ascent, I catch my mind in the act of forming various bear scenarios, each one more violent than the last. The violence comes more from me than from any imagined bear. I realize that as I push myself to keep up my pace despite the altitude gain, something's happening at a physiological, unconscious level—my blood is up. So I breathe it all out. I'll be a mile away from the bear's garbage route. And my food will be hung high, my tent innocent of any smells but my own, which I expect must be distinctly unappetizing after nearly a month on the trail.

A ways short of the summit I find just the spot I'm looking for, a small, solitary tentsite sheltered to the north by a rocky mound. I stake out my feather-light tent carefully, with a stiff western breeze coming up on the unprotected side of the ridge, using all eleven titanium stakes and tightening up each of half a dozen guylines. Then I carry my nearly empty foodbag and my cooking stuff up a short blue blaze spur trail to the top of a steep overlook brooding over my tiny camp. Squatting on a slab of greenstone, I pour simmering water into a packet of freeze dried macaroni and cheese, chew on dried fruit until dinner is ready to eat, and finish up with what's left of my last remaining Fruit and Nut bar. Juncos flit around me, reminding me of my first night above Damascus. As twilight sets in, I can see pinpoints of light at the north end of the valley far below, the outskirts of Waynesboro, where Brian and his car will soon arrive to help me begin the journey home. The breeze grows bone-chilling cold and I pick my way back down in the dusk. I zip myself into my tent and then into my bag, warming up again, and listen to the noises of the juncos scratching the ground, leaves skittering across the rocks, a squirrel or chipmunk approaching and then running away from my tent. The trail is just a few yards above me, but no one has passed since I arrived and no one will pass now that it's dark. I'm alone in the woods and unutterably happy.

Someone asks me, a week later, what I thought about on the trail for those twenty-six days and I have two answers, one of which I usually keep to myself. Here's the other: Food, bears, and bowhunters aside, a lot of my thoughts kept turning on gratitude. Grateful for being able to take this month off, so I could walk north through Virginia in the cool October days. Grateful for the Trail itself and for all those who had helped build and maintain it. Grateful for the leaf change, so much more brilliant than I'd imagined, for the fresh spring water that never gave out, for the birds and animals that played hosts to my visit. Grateful for my health and for the body that never failed me, for all its sixty years of service. Grateful for the long ridges, for the bracing ups, the gentle downs, the farmlands, horse paths, rocks to climb, brooks to soak my feet in. And grateful for everyone who helped me, taking me to the trailhead, taking my maildrops to the post office and tracking them, managing without me, trusting that I'd be OK.

The answer that comes to me just as quickly and that I tend to leave unspoken: harder to put into words. But I'll try. Often what went through my head was nothing like my usual thoughts, which for me tend to form into a steady stream of words, sometimes focused, often random, absurd, frequently obsessive, shot through with emotions and feelings that at times seem to run off on a distinct track of their own. On the trail, though, all this could quiet down and the woods and mountains would do me the great service of thinking for me. The inner monologue peters out and for a time the rocks wordlessly announce their grainy hardness, the trees their sheer rootedness and living wood, the last few stars their cold, vanishing glow. The creek answers with a rush of sound as my boots splash across it, the mud offers its squishiness, the winds pick up their wild inarticulate song. One leaf on the ground next to the trail, its red and yellow streaks vivid against the moss, says everything that ever needs to be said. These don't feel like thoughts. I'm not certain who would be thinking them.

On the back inside cover of the little notebook I carry, along with a few other verses, I've written a line attributed to the Buddha, when a disciple asks him how to reconcile the core truth of "no-self," *anatman*, with the sincere desire to follow the way. Who's there to make the required effort? The Buddha talks about the difficulty of the question, but ends up saying: "For there is a path to follow, and there is walking to be done, and yet there is no walker."

An invitation
in cool mountain solitudes
to no one who walks.

SUMMER (II)

Seeking it yourself with empty hands,
you return with empty hands.

Keizan Jokin, *Denkōroku*

October 2015. A great horned owl hoots commandingly from deep in the woods in the fresh morning light. I wonder if Joni can hear it and realize she's already gone, just a few minutes' walk from the warning sign she'd wanted to see and, I expect, photograph with me next to it. "CAUTION," it reads: "There are no places to obtain supplies or get help until Abol Bridge 100 miles north." Take ten days of food, the sign sternly admonishes, and don't underestimate the difficulty of this section, before dropping the grimly paternal tone to end with a cheery: "Good hiking!"

The trail here is gorgeous and I wish I'd asked Joni to walk a little with me, the sparkling little cascade, the stony brook I hop across dry shod, the sturdy bog bridges spanning patches of sphagnum moss and rich brown mud. The zebra striped hairy woodpecker climbing a tree just to the left of the trail, the ribbon snake slithering across it just ahead. The dense profusion of trees, hemlocks, elephant grey beeches, silver and paper birch, black spruce—though I can hear the trucks on Maine Highway 15 (and will for much of the day) I'm already in the midst of what feels like primeval forest. It's a little after 6:30 on a bright Monday morning and I soon leave any sense of regret behind, feeling energetic and happy to be swallowed up by the thick woods as I pass the first of a whole series of lovely and secluded glacial ponds, each one promising a moose that never appears. It does feel wild in the 100 Mile Wilderness.

The day grows quite warm, topping 70 degrees, by the time the trail winds its way up to the ledges. These soon open to the first views of the hike—miles of dark green forest—and an unexpected treat, rows of scraggly blueberry bushes.

Sun-warmed, untended
ripe wild mountain blueberries
leave some for the bears.

Now gaining altitude (1500 feet over the course of the day), I feel the heft of eight days' food in my backpack, a week's worth for the wilderness and one more day for Baxter Park and Katahdin. Still, I've managed to keep the packload to 32 pounds and within a couple of days I mostly forget I've got anything on my back at all. By mid-afternoon, though, between the overstuffed food bag, the heat, and three tough fords, only knee deep but slippery and treacherous, I feel my mood darken. Especially when, scrambling down to the second ford, my foot slips on a smooth rock and one of my Crocs breaks—a relatively new, fancy pair I bought with the Maine stream crossings especially in mind. I stop at a lean-to for lunch and find a large roll of duct tape someone left, just what I'll need later to try a field repair of the camp shoes, so I wind several feet of it around one of my water bottles. Good thing I take extra, because the second Croc fails in the same way by the time I finish the day's fifteen miles. I tape them back together and then reinforce each strap with orange cord cut from the end of my bear line. That should hold them together until Katahdin.

It looks to be a rainy night and a small crowd starts to converge at Logan Pond Stream lean-to, sited well above said stream and with no pond anywhere in view. Over the next hundred miles I'll leapfrog with a number of the hikers who straggle in, each one mentioning the hard day, as the dark settles and a thunderstorm creeps up on us. A couple of thruhikers, Robot, a lanky German, and Happy, a youthful sixty-five, whose trailname does not belie him. Another long-distance hiker the same age, Grinder, with crew-cut iron grey hair, friendly in his grim way, who's made a cross-generational Trail alliance with a sweet young Montana couple, Newt and Inch King. Coyote, bearded, on the short side, and fit looking—I later learn he won several marathon footraces in California. This group scatters over the next couple of days, and yet I'll end up bumping fists with most of them on the summit of Baxter Peak a week later. (After another bad year of norovirus up and town the Trail, no one wants to shake hands anymore.)

The storms move in and out over the course of a rainy night, clearing up in time for a quiet, luminous dawn, the rain soaking into the ground, the bogs not much boggier than before. But the Wilderness has only begun to show its wild side.

The trail climbs 1700 feet to the ruins of a fire tower on the top of Barren Mountain, with lush views of the ponds below, green hills and mountains rising on all sides with no evident sign of roads or fixed habitations—we are already deep into it. Then down to traverse a classic bog, complete with carnivorous pitcher plants, walking over well-maintained puncheons (single or paired split logs sparing the hiker from a knee deep slog). More classic Maine trail follows, rough hiking over roots and rocks, bog and mud, rarely easy going despite the occasional short stretch of ridge walking, as the trail climbs up and down a series of six low mountains. Ripe blueberries, plots of spruce, hemlocks, beech trees, and on the summits, krumholz—even though the trail rises no higher than 2500 feet.

Around 2:30 in the afternoon thunder again rolls in from the west, distant and occasional at first, but with a cloud stream above rushing in fast. On the way up Chairback Mountain, the last of the day's climbs, I pass an empty lean-to just as the thunder cracks again. Tempting. But I press on, only a few miles from my planned destination, a lonely pond where I hope for a solitary evening.

Toward the north end of the long, rocky summit I come to a dead stop as lightning hits not thirty feet away with no measurable gap between the intense flash of jagged fire and a rollicking boom of thunder. Although it's decidedly uncool to yell in the mountains—others might take it for a distress call—the storm's sudden display of sheer power pulls a whoop of excitement out of my lungs.

A thunderclap just
as ten yards off, forked lightning hits:
a shout of sheer joy.

With no alternative but to move on, I half run toward a stand of trees at the north end of the summit. Just as I reach them the rain comes on, heavy and relentless, as I go through my well practiced routine and pull on hat, rain parka, pack cover, and garbage bag kilt, not quite quickly enough to escape a half soaking. By the time I'm ready to head down the rocky trail, more a vertical quarry than anything like steps, I notice a growing number of pale white objects, the size of grapes or marbles, hitting the ground all around me. An August hailstorm. It comes down thicker and harder, some of the stones the diameter of quarters, and it *hurts*, hitting my head, my hands, my neck, arms, legs—all while I try to negotiate a steep trail now covered with ice chips. A volley of even bigger hailstones starts in and I cry out in pain, immediately hearing someone call out my trailname. It's Robot, who I can now see hunched, almost comically, under some dwarf spruce. I join him at the side of the trail, protected more by my backpack than by the krumholz, as the hail keeps falling for another fifteen minutes.

hail stones like acorns,
we cower under dwarf spruce—
summer mountain storm

Finally it lets up, the air quickly warms, and we head down a trail now heaped with countless little ice balls—it reminds me strangely of winter hiking, although the melting hail makes for surprisingly good, crunchy footing. The boggy stretches now harbor up to a foot of ice water and there's nothing to do but wade through, feet chilled to the bone, boots and socks waterlogged.

A few gentler ups and downs lead finally to a rough side trail and, after a few more minutes, to Chairback Pond. The rain lets up while I stake out my tent on a knoll overlooking the pond, high ground in case the rain starts up again. Instead, the skies begin to clear and mist rolls over the silent pond below. I cook dinner, hang my food, and watch the dusk gather from my sleeping bag, my thin mesh tent door a window over the pond. Now loons swim and dive, hunting in the waning light. Otherwise, no one in sight. Drops of water roll off the rainsoaked leaves above, making a soft tom-tom beat on my tent fly, lulling me to sleep.

The Trail talk keeps coming back to ultra marathoner Scott Jurek, who's just been fined by Baxter State Park for celebrating an unofficial AT speed record on top of Kathadin with an entourage and a bottle of champagne: the Park officials were not amused. There's even a rumor that the northern end of the Trail may be rerouted someplace else. One evening, in a half-filled shelter, I get into an argument over this with a young thruhiker, Tropical. He feels that after more than 2,100 miles on the Trail, he should be able to do whatever he wants at the end: chug a beer, smoke a joint, get naked and shout. I end up saying, more harshly than I mean to, some old guy stuff about respect and not giving AT hiking a bad name. I feel bad about the exchange, partly because I like Tropical, who looks so trail-hardened and, with his shaggy red hair and beard, a little wild himself, going feral after so many months in the woods. More, though, because I didn't manage to make a good case for the wilderness ethic, failing to point out how very, very little of anything that could be called ancient forest is left east, or for that matter west, of the Rockies. (Less than 2 percent of the continental US landmass is protected by the Wilderness Act.) Most of the official wilderness areas in New Hampshire, for example, were once clear-cut—which is no reason not to protect them once they've grown back.

Dirt and gravel logging roads crisscross the 100 Mile Wilderness, as we're all discovering on this trip. Baxter itself, kept largely roadless but with a network of trails and campsites, no longer resembles the dense, nearly impassable forest encountered by Thoreau, who had to start his Katahdin ascent by splashing his way up a rocky streambed.

I regret one moment in particular, where I've tried out a slippery slope argument about finding a concession stand on top of Katahdin, or maybe a chairlift to get tourists up there without the need to climb it. Of course, Tropical scoffs this off. So why didn't I then ask him if he remembered the summit of Mt. Washington? But, morning-after snarky comebacks aside, the question I really want answered is one I wouldn't know quite how to put. How does anyone spend five months on the Trail and not grow to love it, to want to protect it and keep it as intact as possible? Maybe Tropical does love the Trail, just as much as I do, and he simply wants the chance to celebrate it, with a can of good old American lager and a barbaric yawp, when he's completed its tough last mile.

I know the arguments against the whole concept of Wilderness—that it's fake (since roads take you to it and trails get you through it), elitist (since mostly the well-heeled can take advantage of it), that it works against a larger commitment to the environment, with inner city window gardens and grassy highway median strips just as much worth protecting as any subalpine meadow. I can see at least some truth in each of these claims and I also see the big truth they miss. That hiking through areas like Northern Maine or the Smokies, or the Olympic rainforest back in my home state, or even spending half an hour hiking under the ancient hemlocks lining Sages Ravine, gives you an experience of inestimable value, one that can be pointed to but not fully described. If you stay open to it. And you can often see that openness, or the lack of it, in a hiker's eyes. But, I've learned, not always. So I guess I should have just shut up.

Much as I sympathize with the Park's wilderness ethic—and much as I'm disgusted by the speedy trail runner's lack of respect for it—I don't want future hikers to lose the experience I'm having this week. It's hard to imagine a more dramatic and fitting end to the Appalachian Trail, whether for a thru- or section hiker, than the 100 Mile Wilderness and Katahdin. Not only does the northern end feature the toughest, most rugged, and most majestic peak for the final climb, but the wilderness gives a series of Katahdin views as one hikes toward it, each one breathtaking in a different way. Leaving Chairback Pond, first you ford the West Branch Pleasant River, this day through knee-deep water over smooth, slick stones. Then the trail opens up and becomes almost park-like for a time, especially in the neighborhood of Gulf Hagas, an old tourist draw, with the rocks rebuilt into steps for the first steep climb. A series of four rocky peaks, each one growing more rugged and untamed, takes you finally to White Cap Mountain, only 3650 feet high but, as it turns out, high enough. The sky opens up on the summit for fine views to the east of a green jumble of hills, peaks, and jewel-like ponds. And then, moments before the scramble down the north side, something amazing happens.

Fourth of four ascents
White Cap's bare rocky summit
look north: KATAHDIN!

The mountain rises almost due north, huge, unmistakable, dwarfing the lesser peaks in its orbit. For a brief time clouds obscure only the very top. Then all too soon dark clouds gather directly overhead, the view is lost, and the day's sprinkles thicken into a hard, soaking rain. Thunder echoes all around, though this time lightning stays far off. Time for shelter and an early sleep.

The next day brings no new view of Katahdin, as the trail gradually drops into a shallow basin while skirting a new series of ponds—small, lovely Mountain View Pond, big Crawford Pond, Church Pond, Cooper Pond, fjord-shaped Mud Pond. My destination for the night is the final one, Lower Jo-Mary Lake, a large, placid expanse with shallows lined by freshwater mussel shells. As I near it, the forest begins changing, the beeches and paper birches now making room for sugar maple and my old favorite from Massachusetts, goosefoot maple with its broad, jungle sized leaves. I've walked close to twenty miles this day, speeding up over gentle declines, enjoying the ferns that grow here and the eastern junipers that remind me so powerfully of the western cedar trees of my childhood and youth on the other edge of the country.

The rain just keeps holding off and the day's two fords turn out to be easy rock hops, so I arrive at Antler's Campsite, hugging the shores of Jo-Mary, footsore and dry-booted. My tent airs out in the late afternoon sunlight while I dry my socks, which I've draped over some low bushes. I've found a small, private tentsite on a little point with its own five-yard stretch of pebble beach, where I bathe my feet in the sun-warmed pond water, trying not to graze the violet colored mussel shells that line the bottom and flutter with the waves. As I cook dinner, I look out and see a thick, glowing band of electric colors, shaped in a half arch, over the far shore. I've arranged my tent again so that the door looks out over the lake, and I watch the rainbow fade out, chased by a lush sunset as evening comes on. Breezes come off the pond and stir the juniper berries on their way to my tent, giving me distinct whiffs of gin. Soon I'm ready to sleep, loons calling their eerie call as the light fails, and then, after a dreamless night, I awake to hear a hermit thrush singing in the pink light of sunrise.

The next day brings two more views of Katahdin, one totally unexpected. For much of the day the path remains fairly level, but now with tougher going over an endless series of thick roots and slanted rocks. All the twisting steps tear at my feet, blistered by yesterday's long hike in wet socks, but I don't mind it much. The trail follows water today, skirting the edges of lakes and ponds and hugging the banks of brooks and streams. A friendly hiker—Piston?—smiling and hale in his mid-forties, catches me from behind and we walk together a bit. He tells me how he and two friends got trapped in the middle of the Wilderness during Hurricane Irene four years back and, unaccountably, decided just to keep going, slogging through two feet of mud and tag-teaming across chest deep fords. It makes for a great story and the next couple of miles pass quickly. Piston leads me down a short side trail to the north end of Pemadumcook Lake for a perfectly framed view of Katahdin, rising up over green forest beyond the opposite shore, now filling a good part of the horizon, brooding over wood and water. Though the sun has come out (and will mostly stay out for the rest of the trip), a high cloud once again obscures the mountain's very top. I like the slight air of mystery, the way it leaves something still to come.

My chance buddy now powers ahead and again I hike alone, grateful for the solitude, enjoying the water sounds and the cool forest light. Where Namahkanta Stream broadens out into a fair-sized river, I stop and wash out my socks, which have become as stiff as cardboard with all the bog water, then strap them deviously on my backpack to dry out in the sun. (I've seen the occasional fallen sock on the trail over the years, knowing this probably left its owner with only a single intact pair for the rest of the hike.) Then I stop for lunch at the end of long Nahmakanta Lake on a tiny, stony beach where I wash my feet for good measure. There's a lean-to coming up but I feel like going further and getting over the first of the next day's climbs, Nesuntabunt Mountain. The map shows a sweet-looking little tarn not far beyond, Crescent Pond, and I ask a southbounder if he remembers seeing any tent spots there. He's not sure, but he recommends the summit of Nesuntabunt, where there's no water source but room for a single tent if I'm up for some dry camping.

Some fourteen miles from Antler's, where I started, the trail finally climbs a bit, up and down over a couple of sawtooth hillocks before starting the modest climb, just about 700 feet, up Nesuntabunt. Near the bottom I stop at a clear, thin stream snaking from a tiny spring just above, drinking deeply and topping off my water bottles. The climb feels tougher than it should—I must still be tired from the long day before—though soon enough, around 4 p.m., I reach the summit. There's indeed barely enough room for a small tent, but it's too close to the trail. Anyway, there's a side trail to another view of Katahdin, so I follow it through some scrub and out to a rocky point. The skies are clear and the mountain rises up magnificently, centered over Nahmakanta Lake below. Suddenly it feels close, a mere sixteen miles away in a straight line, and for the first time I can see the entire summit, a spiny granite crown topping the highest point in Maine.

Here, too, there's just room for a single backpacking tent and I set up, wondering how much traffic I'll get from others drawn to the view. No one comes by, except for a thoughtful German fellow (not Robot, who by now must be a day ahead of me, but some compatriot) who takes a long look and moves on. I bring my foodsack and backpacking stove onto the rocks for dinner with Katahdin. Below I see small black dots jaggedly moving, disappearing and reappearing on the blue surface of the lake far below—loons diving. Dragonflies whiz by, riding air currents up from the lake, and curious red squirrels flit in and out of the bushes growing hardily out of the rocky soil. With its remote feel, and the view of Katahdin dominating the northern horizon above the beautiful, still lake, I can't help feeling that I've found the single sweetest tentsite on the Appalachian Trail. The air starts to chill around me and I retreat to my tent, angled so it looks out over the lake, to watch the sunset. In two days, with just twenty-five miles of trail to cover before the final big ascent, I'll be at the foot of Katahdin. Tonight there is nothing to desire and nothing to regret. This is what I've come for. There's no place else in the world to be.

The next morning I make breakfast leaning half out of my tent with a sunrise view, a bank of white clouds to the west of Katahdin, orange glowing skies to the east, the great mountain and its entourage of lesser peaks silhouetted against light clouds still further north. The red squirrels are back, more curious than before, as well as a huge hairy woodpecker that diligently works a tree trunk just a few feet away.

One loon swims mid-pond
a black speck, barely in sight—
red squirrels chatter.

Eager to start a longish day, seventeen and a half miles, I pack up and follow the short trail back to the summit where, to my surprise, a fellow backpacker has spent the night. She has set up her tent but slept outside it under the stars; I have to step over her sleeping bag to reach the northbound trail and whisper a quiet good morning, but she either keeps dozing or chooses to play possum. Heading fast down the mountain on easy trail I scare up a ruffed grouse and listen to the loons calling on Nahmakanta Lake. Soon I'm at Crescent Pond, which does indeed boast a nifty little tentsite, though nothing like my mountaintop retreat. Then a view down rugged Pollywog Gorge, a great open wound in the mountain side, followed by a walk along Pollywog stream and a long section along Rainbow Lake, where I hear the unmistakable noise of a wilderness summer camp hidden from view. Again the trail heads steeply up, climbing to Rainbow Ledges and another view point. Walking along the bare rock summit I'm startled by a human voice just behind me. It turns out to belong to Happy, one of the friendly crew from the Logan Pond Stream lean-to on the first night out of Monson. Toward the end of the ledge walk I call Happy over to show him the amazing view that suddenly opens up: Katahdin once more, now looming just ahead of us, huge, glorious, forbidding.

Happy and I walk together, soon reaching Hurd Brook Lean-To, our last stop before Baxter State Park. Tent sites surround the small shelter, with a baseball bat floor, slender pine logs that make me glad I recently splurged on a thicker, yet magically lighter, air pad. One by one, more of the crew from that first night filter in, Newt and Inch King, Grinder, Coyote, and we share stories about the hailstorm and updates on some of the other hikers we've met along the way. It's a reunion. We all have the same plan, to start early and quickly hike the dozen or so miles to the Birches, the tiny campsite reserved for long distance hikers, each of us hoping to nail down one of a strictly limited number of places. The Baxter Park rangers have a reputation, deserved or not, for being rigid to a fault, and the Jurek incident hasn't helped any.

The long day from Antler's, nearly eighteen miles, means I can fall asleep early and keep sleeping hard through the night, despite the excitement that's rippling through the campground. I'm up before six and then hustle to reach the road bounding the Park—the first considerable road I've seen since Monson—

by eight. Although Baxter features what's known as "primitive" camping—no running water except for the streams, no electricity or cell service, minimalist AT-style open lean-tos—the trail through it feels, for the most part, like a walk in the park. The short day (under fourteen miles) and the smooth footing give my ragged toes a needed break before the famously grueling climb up Katahdin. Thanks to several days without rain the two fords turn out to be rock hops, just challenging enough to be fun, though I cross paths with two different southbounders who've each found a way to slip mid-stream and get a soaking before completing their first fifteen miles of the AT. Welcome to Maine!

Even if the water were high today, I'd want these streams forever unbridged. Though the trail passes the occasional maintenance building or parking lot, there's little in the way of mechanical noise and only a few widely spaced road crossings. For the most part it feels like a groomed trail through wild country. I love the way the trail snakes along the big Penobscot River and then climbs with the boisterous Nesowadnehunk Stream, rocky, cascading, uncivilized. The footpath follows their banks through a now familiar mix of hemlocks, eastern junipers, silver and paper birches, with dense stands of bracken and cinnamon ferns. As the trail passes lovely Daicey Pond I think about taking a quick swim, but I want to get to the Birches before more hikers pass me (two young thruhikers have already whizzed by). I know I'm rushing and losing part of the experience but I can't make myself slow down. So I tell myself that if I reach camp early I can finally get my boots off for a long rest before the big climb.

There's no ranger at the Katahdin Stream Campground station when I reach it around noon, so I hike on to the Birches, tucked away out of sight on the other side of an unpaved road. Hare and Honey Badger, the friendly, hyper-fit thruhiker couple who raced by me earlier in the day, have set up on the little site's single tent platform. The two lean-tos—tinier versions of the AT shelters, almost like children's playhouses—stand empty. I lay my gear out in one of the baby lean-tos and head back to the campground and its picnic tables to eat lunch and register for the night. Then I walk along Katahdin Stream, well downstream from the camping spots, find a smooth rock, and lower my legs ankle deep into the frigid water. I let my feet go numb as the ache and the blister pains slowly drain out of them. Then back to the Birches to hang out with a growing crowd of distance hikers, Mouse and Wrecker, another nice twenty-something thruhiker couple, Coyote, Happy and Grinder, and Grinder's young hiking pals Newt and Inch King. Everyone goes to bed early. Katahdin is waiting.

Happy and I are first out the next morning, or so we think, leaving the ranger station by 6 after dropping off our tents, camp shoes, and sleeping pads, lightening our backpacks for the 4100 foot ascent. The morning is clear and I'm totally ready for this last stretch—and a little apprehensive. Katahdin is by far the toughest climb on the AT and more challenging than any of the forty-eight four thousand footers in New Hampshire, all of which I've climbed at least once by now. My feet feel surprisingly solid after a shorter day and a good rest, my knees feel good as always, my legs strong. But my right shoulder is pretty much useless for climbing. Thanks to an after-effect of the long October hike's freak injury to my upper back, coupled with a winter of shoveling through yet another record Boston snowfall, I can't reach overhead without pain or summon much power to pull up. So I take my Leki staff, figuring I can push off with that while I use my left arm to pull. I also stay with Happy, who wants a climbing pal, and this time I'm grateful not to hike alone. For this day, we are fast friends and loyal allies—we'll see each other through.

The first mile or so goes fast, beautiful hiking, a gradual ascent along the ice-cold, crystal-clear waters of Katahdin Stream as they cascade over and churn around an endless jumble of rocks. Once we reach the Falls, after gaining only five hundred feet or so, the trail grows more insistently vertical, though still pleasant enough, as the beech, maple, and hemlocks start to give way to more spruce trees and the ground underneath grows as rocky as the streambed. Now at 2400 feet, some 1300 feet above the trailhead, we reach the last good spring of the hike as above us the rocks grow larger and steeper and the spruce trees begin to dwarf. We've got a great day for it, the sky now blue with mists passing by and a little cloud cover up near the summit, the sun bright and warm. Now the scrambling begins, and edging around one of the first many huge boulders we have to negotiate we're surprised to see someone coming down the mountain, a radiant Honey Badger with Hare close behind. They explain, half shyly, that they started at two a.m. so they could take in the sunrise from the summit. Their faces are still bright with it.

Now we're climbing sheer rock, sometimes diagonally, sometimes side-stepping, sometimes clambering up vertically. I rely on my hands as much as my feet, sometimes hanging my staff from my wrist as I scramble and sometimes using it to push up or off. Without much help from my shoulder I have to improvise at times, at one point using a kind of chimney move to scuttle up to a ledge that Happy has half chinned himself onto. He's amused by my crablike movements and claims to be impressed by my technique, which I expect I taught myself at twelve or thirteen years old, climbing the rocks above my uncle's ranch in Montana. Today I feel intensely aware of what's implicit in every tough ascent, that this climb has every climb I've ever made behind it, in the Whites and the Taconics, in North Carolina and Virginia, and going as far back as the Olympics and the North Cascades—fifty years of mountain karma.

Katahdin, in fact, feels at times like a greatest hits reel of all the toughest and trickiest scrambles from Moosilauke to Monson, along with a few pitches that have no precedent further south. In a very few cases the Park has compromised its wilderness code by chiseling an iron staple or hook into some high, featureless granite slab, which otherwise would stop any climber without technical rock skills and equipment. All done, though, in minimalist style, making it difficult but not impossible to keep going. After forty minutes or so of clambering, we stop for a break on a ledge recessed into the mountainside, stretching out our legs on the sun-warmed rock.

Looking almost due north, though we can't yet see Baxter Peak, our goal, we get a stunning view of the northwestern half of the Katahdin massif. In contrast to most other Eastern mountains, rounded and smoothed by millennia of winds and rains, Katahdin resembles the younger, craggier ranges of the Rockies and points west. We look out to a forbidding profusion of sharp ridges, escarpments and spires that remind Happy of the Sierras and me of the Cascades. The Western feel of the rockscape only intensifies higher up, as the grey stone gives way to more and more red granite, a color that reminds me more of Colorado and Montana than of anything I've seen in the Appalachians. Yet the views that begin to open up to the south and east are pure Maine, miles and miles of seemingly untouched forest, evergreens mingling with the lighter green of hardwoods and underbrush, broken only by silvery ribbons and bright pools of water, the great North Woods as they might have looked to Thoreau in the mid-nineteenth century, or to some nameless mountain wanderer a thousand years before that. Clinging to the rock like beetles, we climb on.

Now we pick our way up a steep ridge toward the Gateway, one more crazy scramble up a rocky shelf leading to the Tableland and the last mile and a half to the summit. Issuing out of the Gateway like a couple of dazed explorers searching for a lost world, we find ourselves at the edge of an alpine landscape that would look totally unearthly if we hadn't seen its likes on the tops of Moosilauke, Washington and a few other high peaks along the way. Short rust-colored grasses, low heather-like groundcover, and everywhere a profusion of lichen-covered rocks. Here and there a scatter of tiny, five-petaled white flowers, diapensia. We stay on a narrow, rocky path, avoiding the fragile alpine plantlife, that takes us to the Thoreau Spring, from which I'd intended to drink deeply in tribute to the greatest of American nature writers. Today, though, it's a shallow, brackish trough and I stick to the unfiltered Katahdin Stream water I've carried up with me, still well chilled despite the morning sun now warming our backs.

From the Tableland we can at last see Baxter Peak itself, a jagged rockpile connected by a sharp arête to South Peak at a second corner of the large summit area. As we head up the gentle incline toward this final ascent, we see the handful of hikers who've passed us over the last hour or so reaching the crest ahead of us, Coyote, still moving fast, a trio of hardy, gung-ho dayhikers doing a reunion climb, Mouse and Wrecker from the evening before, and a plucky family of four I shared a shelter with in the middle of the Wilderness. Soon it will be our turn and, though Happy has been on the Trail for five months and I have for eleven years, we share a single thought: the end is literally in sight. We hike the last twenty minutes to the summit in silence.

I don't believe that spirits guard the higher peaks—aside, maybe, from Mt. Washington in winter—but I do understand why the Penobscots, the Abenakis, and other early Americans held them sacred and tended to avoid them. Thoreau wrote of his own unsuccessful Katahdin ascent, some hundred and seventy years ago, that the "tops of mountains are among the unfinished parts of the globe, whither it is a slight insult to the gods to climb and pry into their secrets, and try their effect on our humanity." (He adds that a Penobscot guide recommended bringing an offering—specifically, a bottle of rum.) Katahdin still has this aura of mystery, at least it does for me this morning, with only a handful of us nearing the rugged crest. The last few yards are nearly overwhelming—not just the sacred feel of the summit, but the emotional freight of eleven years, leaving my marriage, watching Dad die, watching my kids grow up. Watching myself grow up. Happy discreetly turns his head aside as I blink back tears.

And then we're on top. Everyone clicks the requisite photo next to, behind, or on top of the sign marking the "northern terminus" of the AT, 2,178 miles (when the sign was made) from Springer Mountain in far away Georgia. Coyote is broadcasting the Pharell Williams song "Happy" on his iPhone and, after a minute, I quietly ask him to turn it off. Just as quietly, he does and now the silence is broken only by bursts of merry chatter. More hikers begin to arrive—Newt, Inch King, and Grinder, along with a small wave of dayhikers—and I worry a little for the sign as people start clowning on it. So I move away. It's time to visit the cairn. I've brought an offering of my own.

The Katahdin cairn is an imposing, gaunt structure, over ten feet high, a rough pyramid made of stones that have been piled up over decades. As I draw near, all the rocks look local, lichen encrusted versions of the grey and rose tinted granites I've been climbing up and around all morning. I know that some come from further away—thruhikers have been known to carry a few pebbles from Springer to deposit here, and I've heard about rocks brought from as far away as Mount Fuji, mountaineers conveying one great peak's greetings to another. This practice has grown a little controversial, contrary to a strict "leave no trace" wilderness ethic, and for over a decade I've been stricter than most. But the addition I have in mind will remain unseen and will involve no disturbance of the pile, except in some subtle and imperceptible manner.

I move closer to the cairn and the feeling is exactly right. I break out a little tube of medicated ointment (something every backpacker should carry) that I transferred to my packbelt pouch before leaving camp. When Dad died, I stayed with his body while two of his long time aides laid him out, not tearfully but with palpable respect and affection. One of them, Mely, at one point rubbed Dad's ring finger with lotion and slid off the wedding band he'd worn for more than sixty years, handing it to me wordlessly. Wordlessly, I put it on the ring finger of my right hand. It has stayed on ever since, including on all of my hikes. Now I know for certain where it belongs. After a bit of looking I find just the right rift between two of the larger stones, perched over a long flat one. Even with the salve I have to struggle to get it over my knuckle, swollen from summer heat and a week of hiking. Finally it comes off, and I place the narrow gold band on the flat rock—it doesn't weigh much, my parents were barely getting by when they married—and I snap my index finger to flick it in. I hear it go deep into the cairn, caroming down with a series of dull, satisfying clinks. I know that Dad would love this, in the way I know that gravity will keep me from floating off this spot that feels like the top of the world. I turn to take in the view.

Blue still dominates the skies to the south, as though the Katahdin massif itself has stopped the incoming clouds in their tracks (and for all I know, it has). The view into the Wilderness from Baxter Peak had already garnered fame by the time of Thoreau's attempt in 1846. He quotes a still earlier climber's comparison of the same vista to "a mirror broken into a thousand fragments, and wildly scattered over the grass, reflecting the full blaze of the sun." What I see: a huge expanse of pristine greenwood, distant lines of lesser mountains (including some we climbed), and everywhere bright patches of pond and river water reflecting back the sky, some rounded, some ribbon like, some cut by the retreating glaciers into odd shapes like puzzle pieces. And with an overall effect that no one, not even Thoreau, has managed to convey.

Bare rock. Far below,
a thousand glittering lakes—
here is where words stop.

I sit alone among the rocks for awhile, deeply content, wanting for nothing, not even hungry but eating a pemmican bar to keep up my energy for the descent. Time to head down.

Happy and I leave together as the summit starts to fill up with wave after wave of hikers, mostly out for the day but a few we've seen down the Trail over the past week. The summit area and the tableland go by quickly, but the jumble of sharp-edged boulders slows us down again once we pass through the Gateway, and then the tough series of steep granite slabs has us going down almost as slowly as we came up. At a few of the more taxing pitches, where there's only one possible route, we have to wait several minutes as an antlike file of dayhikers makes its way upwards. Half climbing, half dropping down perhaps the trickiest of all—the one with a widely separated bar and hook screwed into the vertical rock—we find a solitary woman perched on the ledge, relaxing. She tells us she decided to let her husband continue on his own—one look at this pitch and her survival instinct kicked in. A little further down we meet two teenage girls who've made the same decision, letting their Dad go on without them. And we pass one athletic-looking young man laid out flat on a ledge, encircled by his hiking buddies and waiting for a ranger with an emergency kit, apparently stricken by an anxiety attack. Katahdin is not for the faint of heart.

Soon enough we're down in the woods again, once more moving quickly, though Grinder must be moving still faster because he catches up with us near the waterfall. The three of us hike together, mostly in silence. I'm struck again by the sheer beauty of these woods, the wild energy of Katahdin Stream, a wildness I feel too in the beating of my heart as we stride down the trail.

About a mile and a half from the trailhead I see a pair of bright, eager eyes looking directly at me, and a wholehearted, all or nothing smile I've come to know well. It's Joni, the high school sweetheart I never had, the true love of my life, here to take me home and hiking up to meet me. My two Trail buddies drop back for a time, then catch us up until Grinder decides to speed ahead. Within an hour we're all in Joni's car, devouring the fruit and sandwiches and potato chips she brought and pulling up at the first roadside market we see once out of the park. Grinder buys Joni and me a pint of Cherry Garcia ice cream and I pick up a couple of six-packs of Long Trail Ale. The celebration starts the moment we stop the car in Millinocket.

Joni and I check into the Appalachian Trail Inn and make dinner plans with some of the gang from the 100 Mile Wilderness—the inn and the streets around it are filled with people I met along the way. I spot Robot lounging in a little park across from the inn, the first I've seen of him since the hailstorm on Chairback. I toss him a can of Long Trail, along with anyone else who will take one. After dinner with most of the hikers I summited with, we sleep in a comfortable, creaky bed and wake up in good time for breakfast at the Appalachian Trail Café, where we find pretty much the same crowd from dinner and say our goodbyes. Soon we'll be back in Boston, only five hours away.

And then what?

EPILOGUE

Carrying my staff across the back of my neck—
going to the thousand, the ten thousand peaks.

Xuedou Chongxian, *The Blue Cliff Record*

May, 2017. Walking south along the ridge I scan for early blossoms, but the past few months have stayed cool and the mountain laurels have scarcely begun to bud. Only a single clump of bluets, pale purple in the sunlight, has sprung up, along with a few flowering dogwoods and a knot or two of witch-hobble, also white-blossomed but with five petals instead of the dogwood's four. No warblers sing, not even an ovenbird, but towhees scrabble in the underbrush, their spring call the sharp, half-whistled "ta-*wheeet!*" that gives them their name. Soon the pines grow low and gnarly and I cross over the smooth summit of Mt. Race, continuing along the ridge, with its wide rustic vista of ponds and pastures opening below. And then the descent, gentle but steady, down into Sages Ravine, its pools and cascades shaded on both sides by towering old-growth hemlocks.

Here I am again.

The plan had been, after Katahdin, to try making at least one overnight trip each month, to keep the legs up, to nurture the wilder reaches of the mind. Returning to favorite stretches of the AT, climbing the New Hampshire peaks by new routes, exploring some of the less travelled paths, where solitude would be easier to come by. And so it went for a time: climbing over Flume and Liberty, the southern peaks of the Franconia Ridge, to tent at Liberty Springs in September; returning to Sages Ravine, a yearly pilgrimage, in October; hiking the mysterious Nancy Brook trail, in November, to spend a frosty night near Norcross Pond; and just managing to follow the unmarked Dry River trail, half-hidden under four inches of fresh snow, through the Dry River Wilderness in December.

The weather took some strange turns after that, heavy snowfalls followed by freakishly warm periods, making for a mid-winter mud season that lasted through February and kept the mountains at bay for a time. And then one day in early March, getting up awkwardly from the ground, something went badly wrong in one knee. Six months after turning sixty I had torn my right meniscus and all hiking stopped for a time.

Months of physical therapy led to surgery which led to still more months of physical therapy until at last, a year and a half after tenting on the frozen ground above the Dry River, the sole human sleeper in a five mile radius, I find myself once more ready for a night in the woods. This time I approach the Laurel Ridge not from the north, at the foot of the steep Jug End, but from the Race Brook Falls trail, cutting three miles off my usual route and landing me on the AT south of Mt. Everett and its tricky descent. I want to test my knee, and also I want my knee to pass.

The Falls prove disappointingly tame as the season has been dry as well as cool, but the steady rain forecast for the next morning should provide a more scenic view of frothy cataracts. The brook running through Sages Ravine, though, already shows plenty of whitewater as it cascades over, around, and down the granite blocks and boulders that litter the gulch. I walk a path that feels familiar and still surprises me, my bare arms and legs going cool as the hemlocks shade out the sun and the temperature drops a good five degrees. My knee feels strong, although my shoulders smart a little under the packstraps. The large campground stands completely empty and I follow the lower path above the brook toward the group site, where I will be able to hear the stream sounds from my tent. I have to improvise my way around two large blowdowns, where a windstorm must have reached peak intensity. I look long and hard before choosing a tentsite, making sure a third tree, or overhanging branch, isn't ready to snap.

Section hiking boasts little of the mystique of thruhiking and it's easy to see why. Unlike hiking the Trail straight through from end to end, it does not lend itself to that oldest and most dependable of story lines: the step-by-step journey of self-discovery, the errand into the wilderness, the unspooling thread of destiny. And yet, by the same token, if section hiking lacks a clearly defined beginning and middle, it never needs to end. Once you have learned how to keep yourself in reasonable hiking shape year in and year out, mentally as well as physically, arranging your life so that it allows for occasional days or weeks away from other pursuits, why ever stop? Backpacking comes to represent not a five- or six-month break from "real" life but an integral part of your life, in some ways the part that feels most real. You've learned how to pack up in an hour or two, how many miles you can cover in various conditions and in a set number of hours, and how to deal with the rain and the cold. Even if a shoulder goes out, as I discovered on Katahdin, you can keep hiking.

And if a knee goes? A year of limping helped me remember, if I needed reminding, that going out into nature could mean stepping out of your front door and walking even a few blocks. Once I could go more than short distances, leaning on a stick or staff, the Charles River bike path waited ten minutes from my house and the Chestnut Hill Reservoir trail stood just as close to my office at school. Not to mention what Ash calls the "urbanature" all around—hawks and falcons flying from the spires of the neo-Gothic buildings on campus, the front gardens dotting my neighborhood in Waltham, the seemingly endless series of animals making their way into Joni's back yard from the woods behind her house, possums, cottontails, raccoons, deer, Rusty (the big feral cat we fed), a stray groundhog, a fisher glimpsed at dawn, a whole family of wild turkeys pecking at the grass. When I could walk two or three miles we would drive to a local park or to an inn in New Hampshire or Vermont to do some light hiking, and my knee got used to climbing again at nearby Prospect Hill Park, a place for chance encounters with foxes and deer and sharp-shinned hawks and once, turning a corner, a coyote nonchalantly crossing the road just a yard or two away. Although I missed backpacking, I don't think of the past year and a half as a time away from the wild things, so much as a time to appreciate how much wildness can be found within and around a large urban area like Boston.

And a stiff knee helped make me conscious as never before that one day my legs may not support me at all. So I find myself thinking back to Dad's last year, when he could no longer manage even with a walker yet still loved to go outdoors. Each day I visited I would wheel him around the perimeter of the eldercare buildings along the narrow beds of evergreen shrubs and grass borders. We always ended up with a long stop at the tiny overlook across the drive, perched on the edge of the West Seattle bluffs. On clear days you could see Mt. Baker due north, distant and bluish white with glacial snow, solitary from this angle and all the more magnificent, the northern sentinel of the high Cascades. "There's Baker," Dad would say. And then, as though remembering it for the first time, he would add, "Didn't you boys climb that once, you and Bri?"

I would answer, "Yeah, Dad, we did," and we would fall back into silence, because nothing more needed to be said, a thousand echoes of two lives spent haunting the high places charging the air between us.

For today, at least, both legs prove sturdy and I've made good time, with lots of daylight left after setting up the tent and hanging a bear bag. I grab my staff and inch down the steep hillside behind the campsite, down to where the brook flows away from the footpath. The little dell feels long untrodden, almost primeval, and the water flows more gently here, running between rocks and along fallen branches caught in the streambed, making its way through the channel the water itself has cut over the centuries, stripping away the soil and revealing the bedrock underneath. A few saplings grow among the bracken fern and, dotted among them, fiddleheads push out of the ground, signs of spring, infant, fairy-looking ferns that will unscroll in another week or two. I rest on a large stone next to the brook, just listening to the flow of the water, hearing its various sounds unravel and grow distinct as it gushes, drips, laps, plops, and trickles its way east toward the Housatonic. Then I clamber back up and explore the campground for a while, still empty when a barred owl starts hooting and I decide to settle in for the night.

After dinner I retreat to the warmth of my tent—a rising wind has cooled the air to the low 40s—and finish reading the dharma book I've brought with me. I fall asleep early, as one does in the woods, and wake at about two in the morning to the sound of light raindrops pattering on the tentfly. As always the sound comforts me, bringing me back to my childhood overnights in the rainy northwest. I can still hear the brook running along its gorge at the bottom of the slope, until the drizzle thickens just enough so that rain and stream sounds mingle together into a fluid blur. Drifting in and out of sleep I lie half conscious and half dreaming for a time, alone and never less alone in the dark of a woodland night, under the ancient trees.

www.ingramcontent.com/pod-product-compliance
Lightning Source LLC
LaVergne TN
LVHW012057160826
845678LV00014B/2860

* 9 7 8 1 7 3 7 5 2 9 9 1 0 *